Emmerdale
Behind the Scenes

Emmerdale
Behind the Scenes

ANTHONY HAYWARD

ORION

YORKSHIRE
TELEVISION

First published in 1998 by Orion Media
This paperback edition published 1999
An imprint of Orion Books Ltd
Orion House, 5 Upper St Martin's Lane, London WC2H 9EA

Emmerdale © Yorkshire Television Limited
Text copyright © Anthony Hayward/Profiles 1998
Production photographs © Yorkshire Television Limited 1998
Set and Harwood photographs © Derry Brabbs 1998

A CIP catalogue record for this book is available
from the British Library.

ISBN 0–75281–857–0

Printed and bound in Italy

Contents

Acknowledgements

Many people have helped me in my research and I would like to thank the following: current *Emmerdale* producer Kieran Roberts and former producer Mervyn Watson; *Emmerdale* production controller Timothy J. Fee, who pointed me in the right direction and opened all the right doors; *Emmerdale* production designer Mike Long, who spent many hours taking me around both the outdoor set at Harewood and the studio sets at the Emmerdale Production Centre, as well as giving me detailed information on all of the serial's houses and other properties; *Emmerdale* archivist Helen Watson, who endured an unending flow of questions and checked the storyline details; producer's secretary Wendy Bloom; Tim Worsnop, Giles Latham and Sue Youll in the *Emmerdale* press office; Emmerdale Production Centre receptionist Julie Bywell; Yorkshire Television stills librarians Andrea Pitchforth and Rose Wheatley; Richard Thorp; Creskeld Hall; and Rudding Park. Thanks must also go to Derry Brabbs for his superb photographs, Trevor Dolby and Natasha Martyn-Johns at Orion Media and my wife, Deborah.

Anthony Hayward

Foreword

Yorkshire Dales village a short distance from Leeds – that was the unlikely reality created on the Harewood estate when *Emmerdale* started shooting its outdoor scenes on a purpose-built set away from the hordes of tourists who had often held up shooting in the past. In 1998, the popular ITV serial could boast this remarkable backdrop while continuing to enjoy its phenomenal success of recent years, attracting audiences of up to 14 million.

For the first time in its quarter-century screen history, *Emmerdale*'s pub, shop, tearooms, houses, vet's surgery, village institute, churchyard and cricket pavilion were contained together in a fictional television setting that had been turned into reality. Whereas many of the buildings had previously been filmed separately without the geography of their real-life location matching that of the fictional village, the new, lifelike outdoor set was constructed in meticulous detail to resemble what had previously existed only in the minds of producers, actors and viewers.

This book presents, for the first time, an in-depth account of the fascinating building project at Harewood, masterminded by production controller Timothy J. Fee and production designer Mike Long, and takes readers on a tour of all the village's buildings – combining the fictional history of each with a revealing insight into the real-life studio and outdoor sets.

The chapters on the *Emmerdale* properties each begin with a listing of characters from the serial who have lived there, and the dates they did so. If the properties' inhabitants have not been featured on screen at a particular time, these dates are omitted. So, for instance, as the shop and post office was not seen for many years, the listing is for only those years when the building and its inhabitants did appear.

The Making of a TV Village

After 25 years of filming outdoor scenes first in Arncliffe and then in Esholt, surrounded by tourists, Emmerdale *faced the task of constructing its own, purpose-built village.*

The brief was simple: to find the most effective way of making *Emmerdale* as it increased its weekly output to three half-hour episodes, plus occasional hour-long specials. That was the challenge facing the programme's production controller, Timothy Fee, just before *Emmerdale* entered 1997, its 25th-anniversary year. Most outdoor filming for the serial's two weekly episodes had taken place in the West Yorkshire village of Esholt for the previous 20 years, following almost four years in picturesque Arncliffe, in Littondale. But Esholt's reputation as 'the village where *Emmerdale* is filmed' meant that it attracted tourists, causing problems for Yorkshire Television in filming there.

'Arncliffe was a lovely location, but an awfully long way away,' says Tim, who worked on early episodes of the serial as a floor manager and who has been in his current job since 1989, responsible for the logistics of making the programme and running the Emmerdale Production Centre. 'We had to bring the village closer to our production base in Leeds for practical reasons. There was too much time spent in travelling to Arncliffe and it's very expensive to put the cast and crew up in overnight accommodation.

'So the search went on for a Dales village in Leeds, which is quite difficult. Eventually, somebody stumbled on the village of Esholt, between Leeds and Bradford. It was built years ago by the Yorkshire Water Board, which had a huge waterworks there and needed houses for its workers.

'Once the phenomenon of tourists visiting television locations started, perhaps with *All Creatures Great and Small*, Esholt became a target. It was very easy for the tour operators to visit because it cost them nothing to go there. They could drive a coach to the village, park it on the street and put down their travellers, who spent no money and were of no benefit to the villagers, nor to us. They had a lovely day, but we and the villagers suffered.

'In 1989, I actually stood in a field with the executive producer, Keith Richardson, and looked at a possible site for the building of a village set at

Opposite Location filming for Emmerdale *originally took place in the picturesque Littondale village of Arncliffe.*

Above In 1976 outside filming switched to Esholt, near Bradford, to be closer to Yorkshire Television's studios in Leeds.

Rudding Park, near Harrogate, which we had started using as the location for Frank Tate's Holiday Village and various barns and other farm buildings. That site never came to fruition as a place to build a village for many reasons, one of which was that at that point the tourism problem in Esholt wasn't bad enough to warrant the investment that would have been needed in building an outdoor village set. But I had a vision that day.'

At that time, Tim was more concerned with setting up *Emmerdale*'s first production centre, at a converted woollen mill on four floors in Farsley, a few miles outside Leeds, after 17 years of erecting and dismantling interior sets on a weekly basis at Yorkshire Television's studios in the city. But Tim kept his vision in the back of his mind, until the day came when fate made a purpose-built outdoor set a necessity.

The Emmerdale village set at Harewood

The set consists of the following buildings:

Old School Tea Rooms *Kathy Glover, Eric Pollard (business downstairs, flat upstairs)*

Tenant House *Biff Fowler, Marlon Dingle, Will Cairns*

Jacob's Fold *Unoccupied*

Dale View *Unoccupied*

Connelton View *Unoccupied*

Victoria Cottage *Kathy Glover and Alice Bates*

Keepers Cottage *Seth Armstrong and Betty Eagleton*

Post Office and Village Stores *Vic and Viv Windsor*

Mill Brook/Croft Cottage *Unoccupied*

Smithy Cottage/Vet's Surgery *Zoë Tate*

Oak Lea *Unoccupied*

Mulberry Cottage (B&B) *Unoccupied*

The Grange *Unoccupied*

The Woolpack *Alan Turner and Terry Woods*

Pear Tree Cottage *Steve and Kim Marchant*

Woodbine Cottage *Unoccupied*

Tug Ghyll *Unoccupied*

Dale Head Farm *Lisa Dingle's car-repair workshop*

Mill Cottage *Rachel Hughes and Joseph Hughes*

Farrers Barn *Accommodation unoccupied/Barn used for Eric Pollard's antiques business (downstairs) and Mandy Dingle's secondhand clothes shop (upstairs)*

Ford Cottage *Unoccupied*

Beck Cottage *Unoccupied*

Village Institute

Churchyard

Cricket Pavilion

War Memorial

Bus Stop

Buildings used for the Glovers' former house at Holdgate's Farm and the Dingles' residence, Wishing Well Cottage, are visible about 500 yards away from the village set. The real-life Burden Head Farm, used for filming exteriors of Emmerdale Farm, is 1½ miles away, next to the entrance to the *Emmerdale* site at Harewood. Creskeld Hall, where Home Farm exteriors and a few interiors are shot, is about another mile away. Rudding Park, used for filming the Holiday Village, is a little further away, on the outskirts of Harrogate.

The fictional Woodside Farm, which the Cairns family renovated after buying it from Jack Sugden, was another location – Carr House Cottages – on the Harewood estate, but this ceased to be used after the family left the serial in 1998.

And Then There Were Three...

Matters came to a head when, in 1996, the ITV Network Centre asked Yorkshire Television to make a third weekly episode of *Emmerdale*, which had by then increased its viewing figures to more than 13 million, making it regularly one of the three most popular programmes on television.

'I was asked what problems that would present me with and what I would need to make that number of programmes,' recalls Tim. 'You could argue that it was only one extra episode a week – six programmes to be made in every two-week production cycle instead of four – but it totally doubled our production. It meant using two crews instead of one, with the result that visits to Esholt were twice as many.

'The years had rolled by and the tourists flocked into Esholt in increasing numbers. The joke was that we used to pride ourselves on never revealing the name of the village where we filmed, but the Bradford Tourist Board actively promoted Esholt as the place where *Emmerdale* was filmed and *we* got all the hassle from the villagers.

'I could see this huge problem looming on the horizon, with the production teams constantly being surrounded by tourists invading the privacy of villagers and spending more time politely asking tourists to move, to be quiet during "takes" and not to take photographs.

'To film the programme, we also had to request residents to move their cars or turn off the engines, take in their washing and switch off their televisions, as well as asking whether they minded us putting lights in their bedrooms. When you actually added up all of the time spent doing that, it meant that you lost almost half a day's filming a week.'

Tim approached Yorkshire Television's then managing director, Bruce Gyngell, with the dream that he had had years earlier – that of creating a purpose-built village in a controlled environment, away from the public. He was given the go-ahead to find a suitable site and get the scheme costed.

'As the discussions went on, it came down to a simple equation: how much we were losing by continuing to film in Esholt against how much it would cost to build our own village,' recalls Tim. 'At that time, we were actively involved with the Harewood estate, outside Leeds, which provided us with the Dingles' and the Glovers' houses, and filming of farm buildings had moved there from Rudding Park, which saved us half-an-hour a day in travel time.

'Although several other locations were considered, including Rudding Park, Ripley Castle and Creskeld Hall – where Home Farm is filmed – the Harewood estate came up with a possible site for a village. Eventually, that one proved impossible because it was too close to the heart of the estate and they decided it should not be developed. But we then identified a more suitable site, a huge cornfield on the southern fringes of the estate, across the road from the Dingles and Glovers.

'We worked on the business plan in 1996 and put together the planning application that went to Leeds City Council the following year. That was quite a difficult period because it had to be done

Emmerdale established its own production centre at a converted woollen mill in Farsley in 1989.

In the Studio

All indoor scenes were originally recorded at Yorkshire Television's main studio centre in Leeds when *Emmerdale* began life as *Emmerdale Farm* in 1972. Sets were erected and taken down as needed, with a maximum of four up at any one time. These indoor scenes were recorded over two days every two weeks.

In 1989, the first self-contained Emmerdale Production Centre was established in a converted woollen mill at Farsley, a few miles outside Leeds. This came a year after the serial started to be shown every week of the year for the first time in its history, creating the need for more studio space.

The £2-million, purpose-built production centre occupied four floors, the middle two containing permanent studio sets. Lightweight, hi-tech microchip cameras were also used for the first time, and four episodes were made over every two-week period, the first week spent on location and the second in the studio.

With an increase to three episodes a week in 1997, *Emmerdale* needed more studio space. As a result, the production centre moved in November 1996 to Burley Road, in Leeds, a short distance from Yorkshire Television's main studio complex.

Also, schedules were changed so that two separate directors and production crews each recorded three episodes over two weeks, each normally spending five days on location during the first week and two-and-a-half days in the studio the next week.

With the prospect of three episodes a week to record, cast and crew moved to a new production centre in Leeds, near Yorkshire Television's main studio complex.

properly. We couldn't afford to get it wrong – the Harewood estate couldn't and nor could the city council.

'Very difficult negotiations went on. They weren't acrimonious, but productive. Planning permission was granted in June 1997, with the proviso that no permanent dwellings would be built, and the bulldozers moved in during the early part of August. The building of the village – plywood houses clad with Yorkshire stone – took 20 weeks, which was an amazing feat of construction considering there were 22 houses, a pub, a tearoom, a post office, a vet's surgery, a village institute, a cricket pavilion, a churchyard and a bus stop.'

Tim's vision had become a reality, at a cost of £3 million for an entire village. The cast and crew bade farewell to Esholt in December 1997 and filming in the amazingly lifelike new 'village' began on 13 January 1998. The first scene, shot outside The Woolpack, was broadcast on 17 February 1998.

For Tim, the project was one of the most exciting of his working life. 'I haven't taken anybody to the village who hasn't said, "Can I move in?"' he enthuses. 'It's the most unreal experience. This is not *Coronation Street*, *Brookside* or *EastEnders*. This isn't even Burbank Studios, Los Angeles. This is the village built on the edge of Leeds in 20 weeks that will win the Dales Village of the Year Award because that's what it is – a *real* village.'

DESIGNS ON CREATING REALITY

The task of planning and overseeing the outdoor village set fell to production designer Mike Long. 'I like the location we settled for,' says Mike, 'because it centralises our filming base. The Glovers' and the Dingles' were always, in story terms, half a mile or so out of the village. In filming terms, although I haven't built them this distance away, they do look it on camera.

'We took over a big, triangular field and put the village in the bottom corner of it. We've planted meadow wild flower and grass mix, and eventually hope to put sheep in there from one of the farms

on the Harewood estate – in fact the one we use for filming Emmerdale Farm itself in the programme. I just want to get animals around the village, because in the Dales they are very much a part of villages.

'Having settled on the site, I had to redesign the village because it's a different shape, the trees are in a different place and there is a river running through it. So I had to build a road and a bridge over the river, as well as a ford.

'There wasn't a church in our original scheme, but I felt the lie of the land meant it was crying out for one. When it was re-costed, various items were crossed out, including the church, which would have cost £165,000. As a result, we also lost the vicarage. So all we have is a churchyard and I hope that some time in the future we might get a church.

'I then had to come up with accurate designs for all of the 28 buildings so that we could apply for planning consent. Those drawings were completed in the summer of 1996 and handed over to the

Above The building of the new outdoor Emmerdale village set at Harewood, near Leeds, was the result of production controller Timothy Fee's behind-the-scenes diplomacy and production designer Mike Long's creativity.

Below Kim Marchant's first husband, Frank Tate, and dead lover, Dave Glover, are buried close to one another in the village graveyard, which has no nearby church after this was struck from designer Mike Long's plans, to save money.

As in real-life Dales villages, some Emmerdale *houses have dates carved in large stone lintels above the doors.*

architects. At that time, we were switching studios from Farsley back to Leeds, so I was able to concentrate on the job of redesigning those sets, with the help of assistant designer Teresa Clayton. During that period, I also found a new location for Emmerdale Farm at its present site, next to the road leading to our site at Harewood.

'Then, from about Easter 1997, the village started to materialise. Before planning consent came through in June, we had permission to do some exploratory works. So we appointed a contractor, Totty Construction of Bradford, who found five very large water mains pipes side by side, supplying the north Leeds area, together running 66ft wide diagonally across the field, very close to the surface, which no one had told us about.

'I hurriedly had to re-lay the village so that this swathe of pipes could go between the buildings because I wasn't allowed to put anything on top of them. Eventually, we managed to get permission for part of the road to go over the pipes. There was

a lot of legal wrangling with Yorkshire Water, but that was finally sorted out.

'We also had to move an overhead power cable that went diagonally across the site by diverting it parallel to a boundary wall, then burying it underground.'

Once planning consent was obtained, work began on the 28 buildings – all very different from one another – roads and drainage. Only one access point was allowed into the site over the pipes, so a huge concrete raft was built over them that would stand the weight of the production team's lorries and equipment. Restrictions on the width meant that this raft could allow only one-way traffic. The stream running through the site was dammed at two points to form weirs.

Mike kept a close eye on the building work throughout. 'I made a few minor adjustments as it progressed,' he recalls. 'There were, for example, several level changes. A floor level was set in Zoë Tate's cottage and digging started. Just before the concrete was poured, I decided it needed to be 3ft higher. If I hadn't been on site all the time, those subtleties would not have been picked up.'

By Christmas Eve 1997, the construction work was almost finished. 'We all went off for Christmas feeling pretty good about it,' says Mike. 'It was an amazing achievement.'

A Dales Village

Mike's brief from the producer Mervyn Watson was to make the outdoor set look like a Dales village, not like Esholt, north of Bradford, where *Emmerdale* had been filmed for 21 years. But the geographical relationship between the post office, the pub, and the three cottages belonging to Betty Eagleton and Seth Armstrong, Kathy Glover and Steve Marchant had to remain. Everything else was open to Mike's creative imagination.

The Designer

Production designer Mike Long, who was responsible for creating *Emmerdale*'s outdoor village set at Harewood, worked on early episodes of *Emmerdale*, when location scenes were filmed in Arncliffe and interiors were shot at Yorkshire Television's Leeds studios.

'The first designer on the programme was Geoffrey Martin, who was Yorkshire Television's head of design but is, sadly, no longer with us,' recalls Mike. 'He set up the first studio in the company's main complex and I remember the sets going in there for the first time. I did one or two episodes over the years but spent most of my time making film dramas such as *Harry's Game*, the *Beiderbecke* series, *Stay Lucky* and *A Touch of Frost*.

'In 1995, I was between programmes and was asked to go to *Emmerdale* to be an overall production designer, which they'd never had before – they'd only had designers working on blocks of episodes. This was shortly after Mervyn Watson arrived as producer and my task was to improve the studio sets in the Emmerdale Production Centre at Farsley, where the programme had been based since 1989, because they had all got very sad and tired over time, and to do the same with some of the locations.

'We were, for example, having trouble with the Emmerdale Farm location – the second one in the programme's history, called Hawthorn Cottage in the script – which wasn't very visual.'

Filming of outdoor scenes in the village had moved from Arncliffe to Esholt in 1976. With the prospect of *Emmerdale* being screened three times a week, the programme needed to increase its studio space and move its filming locations closer together to ensure that no time was wasted travelling between them. The first objective was achieved when the cast, production team and administrative staff left their self-contained Farsley studios and moved to a new complex in Burley Road, Leeds, a short distance from Yorkshire Television's main studios, in November 1996.

The then Prime Minister, John Major, opened the new Emmerdale Production Centre in January 1997, just over two months after work on the programme had moved there from Farsley.

'As the go-between for the architects and Tim Fee, I was involved in how we laid out that building, particularly the studio space, and in redesigning some of the sets, adapting others and putting one or two new ones in,' says Mike. 'That had to happen within a two-week period in October 1996 when there was no studio recording to be done. It was a 24-hour-a-day, 14-day process and was up and running by the end of that month.'

Designing a purpose-built village set on the Harewood estate, away from the tourists who flocked to Esholt, was an even greater challenge that had still to be met.

'The houses are not that different from those in Esholt in terms of feel, proportions, shape and size,' says Mike. 'For instance, Betty's door and windows are in the same position – I've just given her better windows and a nicer door. In Esholt, we were using people's houses because that's where we wanted to film, but the front door belonged to the person who lived there. If we didn't like it, we just had to put up with it. Now, I've been able to give Betty a front door that I think is a bit more interesting.

'Also, the stonework in Esholt is sandstone and a very black grit stone laid in courses – it's a little industrial village, quite pretty but not of the Dales. I wanted to introduce architecture that you would get in the Dales to make the houses look as if they had been here for 300 years or whatever.

'My assistant, Teresa Clayton, and I spent weeks scouring the whole of the Dales until we decided on an area that we felt was a nice colour and had a friendly feel. We didn't copy any villages, but we copied a few buildings. The area goes from Linton, just south of Grassington, through Conistone and up to Kettlewell. They are all in a line and those are the four villages that I continually went back to, taking hundreds of photographs. I took a stonemason out there to look at walls and chimneys, and the details of the buildings generally, so that we could use some of that in our village.

'The stonework in those Dales villages has a rubble limestone effect – different shapes of stone all over. That gives the buildings externally a very different effect to anything that is coursed. All the corners of the buildings have very large stones called quoins, so we had to create that in some way. Most of the window and door surrounds have large stone lintels, vertical surrounds and mullions, some shaped, some square. I wanted to re-create that, too.

'Originally, we felt that the only way we could afford this was to do it artistically, using breezeblocks for the buildings with a rendered finish sculpted by scenic artists to look like stone. In fact, we found a company that could do it and they did samples. Although they made an excellent job of it, we were never 100 per cent confident. It was very

much in the hands of a tradesman who on a bad day might do a bad job but on a good day might be all right. We were talking about a whole village, so we were very nervous.

'The sum of money that the firm had quoted went into the budget, and when Totty's were appointed to do the building work they were not happy about the thought of doing this. So they agreed to build that effect in real stone for the same amount of money. We jumped at it!

'Although I envisaged building everything out of breezeblock with the stone cladding, this would not have been possible in the given time. The contractors decided to use a timber-frame method of construction. They had a contact who was responsible for a lot of timber-frame buildings around the country and decided to use that contact's professionalism and speed of construction to do the village.

'As a result, we have 28 timber-framed structures wrapped in Yorkshire stone – limestone rubble. We've used a little bit of sandstone in with the limestone just to give a variation of colour, and the tearooms are built out of just sandstone to vary the feel of the village.

'The quoins are gritstone and the stone surrounds to the windows and doors are gritstone where they are square-cast. But where we have anything that is architecturally shaped, such as shaped stone-mullioned windows or a few door lintels with dates carved in them, we have cast it in artstone, which is a very fine, dense concrete. Then we've "distressed" it by sandblasting, which takes all the sharp edges off. A scenic artist then worked on all these with stainers to make them look old.

'The roofs are built out of what looks like Yorkshire slate but they are, in fact, very good concrete reproductions. We've used three different "ages" – different colours, different sizes, different thicknesses – to vary the effect on some of the roofs. We've also built in a few roof "sags" and broken a lot of tiles and repaired them with cement so that they all look of a different age.'

Some of the buildings in the village have been made to look up to 400 years old. Mike was

*The timber-framed structures at Harewood are
covered in Yorkshire stone – limestone rubble – with a
bit of sandstone to give a variation of colour.*

A Historic Site

The *Emmerdale* village set is on the Harewood estate, near Leeds, but well away from the palatial Harewood House, home to the Lascelles family since the 18th century. Most of the house was built in the 1770s when the first Lord Harewood, Edwin Lascelles, hired architect John Carr to oversee the work and commissioned Robert Adam to design the interiors and Thomas Chippendale to make the furniture. 'Capability' Brown supervised most of the landscaping of the formal parks at Harewood.

The estate comprises various farms rented out to tenant farmers, a system that proliferated in Beckindale during the early years of *Emmerdale*. The nearby model village in Harewood has terraces of elegant, dark-stone houses, also designed by Carr, Yorkshire's most celebrated architect.

The estate is now run by the seventh Lord Harewood's eldest son, David Lascelles, a producer who made two series of *Inspector Morse*, *The Fortunes and Misfortunes of Moll Flanders* and Ian McKellen's film version of *Richard III*. Parts of the estate have been used for filming scenes in *Heartbeat* and *A Touch of Frost*.

When Leeds City Council granted planning permission for the *Emmerdale* village set to be built, one of the conditions was that local labour – for jobs such as security and gardeners – should be used. These people are employed by the Harewood estate.

The village is built on green-belt land, so the council also stipulated that no permanent dwellings could be built – all the houses are classed as 'temporary structures' – and tourists are not allowed on the site. The planning permission lasts 10 years before it has to be renewed.

adamant that every house should have a name, instead of some of the cottages being numbered, as previously. This, he points out, is what you will find in most Dales villages.

Once the building work was completed, the houses' walls and roofs were coated with yoghurt both to 'age' them down and attract moss and algae to grow on them. This work was not completed by the time filming began on the outdoor set in January 1998, so priority was given to those buildings whose exteriors are most commonly seen in the programme, such as The Woolpack, the post office, the vet's surgery and the tearooms.

All the buildings in the *Emmerdale* village are used for exterior filming only, apart from the vet's surgery and village institute, which contain interiors. However, most of the buildings have entrance halls decorated so that cameras can show an illusion of the interiors.

Gardens

Building a 'village' from scratch allowed designer Mike Long to include back gardens that have never previously been seen in the serial. 'I wanted all the gardens to look different because they belong to different people,' says Mike. 'For instance, Betty's is all hollyhocks and windowboxes and huts for the birds. Whenever you saw Betty leaving her house before, she was always coming out of the front door. Now, she can go into the back garden and Seth can be tending his marrows in his greenhouse.'

Landscaping and trees were needed to make the village's surroundings look real. 'All the trees were imported,' says Mike. 'The largest one, on the grass next to the public telephone box outside the post office, is a big oak tree that came from Germany. There are also two more big oak trees, a horse chestnut and lime.' Landscaping continued for a few weeks after filming began on the outdoor set because rainy weather from mid-November to the end of December 1997 had stopped some of this work.

Empty Houses

Twelve 'empty' houses were also built, giving a sense of reality to the village and providing opportunities

For the first time, Emmerdale viewers have been able to see villagers' back gardens since the purpose-built outdoor set was created at Harewood.

for the writers to introduce new characters or move around existing ones. A cottage, The Grange, was built on to the side of The Woolpack. There are also two empty houses – Mulberry Cottage (with a B&B sign) and Oak Lea – next to it at the end of the main street. The B&B has a '1656' date stone above the door. Artstone was used for door surrounds and black stone-mullioned windows.

On the other side of the main street, Connelton View is empty. It was built in the same style as the other houses in that terrace, belonging to Kathy Glover and Seth Armstrong and Betty Eagleton. Next to it are Dale View and Jacob's Fold, which adjoins Tenant House (previously known as 'Annie's Cottage'). There are also two semi-detached workers' cottages on the other side of the stream, a short distance from the village green and cricket pavilion. Access is through a ford that Mike and his team created. The stream itself is dammed at the end, a short distance away.

Facilities

A new road was built on the site, as well as a hump-back bridge and ford over the stream. A bus stop is situated at the top of the village, which is geo-graphically similar to Esholt. Next to it is a road sign indicating 'Hotten 7½' and 'Connelton 2¾'

in one direction and 'Robblesfield 3' in the other.

There is mains electricity and a massive septic tank for a waste system. The only buildings on the new village set to be heated are those used for interior filming – the vet's surgery and village hall – and the terrace of four, starting at Steve and Kim Marchant's cottage, that are used as the Green Room, toilets, costume, make-up and designer's offices, and a security office with radio contact to Harewood House.

The site – about one mile inside the Harewood estate – has seven security cameras and two guards on duty around the clock, one in the security office watching the pictures from the cameras, the other patrolling.

In addition, there are sockets around the 'village' so that the production team's equipment can be plugged in, the tungsten street lights can be dimmed and each give out a shaft of light, whereas ordinary ones give an outward beam. Chimneys can produce smoke at the press of a button on a computerised control panel hidden away with other electrical equipment in the barn at Dale Head Farm, which is the setting for Lisa Dingle's car-repair business in the serial. 'Most telephone wires are false,' adds Mike Long, 'although a real one goes to the security office.'

Five hundred yards away from the 'village' is a facilities centre – designed to look like an agricultural building so that it can be seen in the background of some shots on screen – that houses a canteen and changing rooms. Behind it is a car park.

A New Panorama

The *Emmerdale* village set at Harewood has given the serial a refreshing new look, and directors of the programme have been provided with new possibilities. 'We could take shots from a helicopter looking down and see all sorts of things going on because I've given them a 360-degree panorama of village life,' says Mike. 'Before, we've had only small snatches of Esholt. It's so visual on the new set that directors won't be able to stop themselves panning out and filming wide shots of the village.'

Changes to the look of houses have had to be reflected in the studio sets at the Emmerdale Production Centre in Leeds. 'I had to change doors and windows to match what was built at Harewood,' says Mike. 'I also repainted all the backcloths in the studio so that they are of our new "village", not Esholt.'

When new producer Kieran Roberts took over in March 1998, he was well placed to offer an outsider's view of the project at Harewood that was the result of Tim Fee's careful negotiating skills and Mike Long's creativity.

'It's the first time I've ever seen a set that I actually wanted to live in,' he says. 'It's an enormous achievement, both creatively and technically – a fantastic piece of design and a fantastic piece of building. As producer, it's a wonderful facility to have inherited.'

Timetable for Outside Set

The timetable for the building project at Harewood was:

DECEMBER 1995
Announcement that Emmerdale *is to be broadcast three times a week. Production controller Tim Fee has already been working out how this can be achieved. Talks have taken place about increasing space at the* Emmerdale *Production Centre in Farsley or finding a new base. Consideration is given to increasing the production team size and centralising location filming. Tim's dream of building* Emmerdale*'s own village set is now close to reality. The search for a site begins and costings are formulated.*

JANUARY/FEBRUARY 1996
Harewood is chosen as the best logistical location to centralise production. A site at the heart of the Harewood estate is proposed by estate director Christopher Ussher. Emmerdale *production designer Mike Long surveys the site, then designs first prototype village set, which is costed and approved by the Yorkshire Television board.*

MARCH 1996
The Harewood estate has second thoughts about the site. Mike and Tim set about investigating alternative sites. After further discussions with Christopher Ussher, the field opposite the locations already used on the estate for the Dingles' and the Glovers' homes is identified and agreed with the estate. This site will centralise all production around one base.

APRIL 1996
Mike redesigns church and vicarage, a new model is completed and discussions with architects begin. A new site for the Emmerdale *Production Centre is also identified and costed on the Harewood estate. However, this exercise proves impractical from a financial and planning point of view and is replaced with a plan to move studios from the converted mill at Farsley to Burley Road, a short distance from Yorkshire Television's main studio complex. Increased costs are identified on the new site at Harewood and the church, vicarage and some landscaping items are omitted from the new scheme.*

MAY 1996
Mike designs new studio layout for Burley Road. Tim starts to plan the move from Farsley to Burley Road.

JUNE 1996
Full planning application deposited with Leeds City Council on 11 June 1996. Mike pursues discussions about the building of the village in terms of rendering timber-frame structures clad in stone. Board approval granted 29 June. Mike completes working drawings of all properties in the village between 27 June and 12 September. Specifications and bill of quantities prepared by the architects, Building Design Partnership of Manchester.

AUGUST 1996
Work begins on the new studio complex at 27 Burley Road.

SEPTEMBER 1996
Contract for the building of village at Harewood goes out to tender on 12 September.

OCTOBER 1996
Tenders received and assessed. Totty Construction of Bradford is appointed. Production facilities and studio sets move from Farsley to Burley Road. Location shooting continues in Esholt. Not a day of production is lost in the move.

NOVEMBER 1996
Studio move completed in three weeks. By 10 November, the interior sets and technical equipment have been moved in their entirety, re-erected and tested, and run without a hitch. Shooting begins. Totty Construction suggests that the outdoor set at Harewood can be built out of real Yorkshire stone for the same cost as proposed rendering.

JANUARY 1997
Prime Minister John Major officially opens the new Emmerdale *Production Centre at Burley Road. Totty Construction prepares sample panels for Mike Long to investigate the look of the stone.*

MARCH 1997
New Emmerdale Farm interior set built in the studio. Proposed starting date for Harewood outdoor set planned for April, subject to planning permission.

APRIL 1997
Discussions take place between Yorkshire Television and Yorkshire Water about mains pipes running directly under the proposed village.

MAY 1997
Method of protection for mains water pipes running under village finally agreed.

JUNE 1997
Planning permission granted. Totty Construction moves onto the site to prepare the site compound, build new access road and generally set out site.

JULY 1997
Still awaiting legal agreement with Yorkshire Water regarding village site area passing over mains pipes. Agreement signed on 30 July.

AUGUST 1997
Concrete bases poured, timber frames arrive and erection of buildings begins.

SEPTEMBER 1997
Village telephone box arrives! Cairns cottage completed on a site away from the village set but still on the Harewood estate. Filming begins there on 11 September.

OCTOBER 1997
Mike Long gets smoke machines after Tim Fee's careful negotiations with Yorkshire Television accountants. Wooden footbridge installed. Main road through the village constructed early so that it will 'distress' by the time filming begins. Landscaping starts.

NOVEMBER 1997
Telephone poles erected. Lots of rain!

DECEMBER 1997
Christmas looms and the finish deadline is in sight. The contract finishes in 20 weeks, just two weeks over the original estimate of 18 weeks.

JANUARY 1998
Director Tim Dowd directs first scene on new outdoor set in front of The Woolpack, on 13 January.

FEBRUARY 1998
First scenes from outdoor set screened 17 February.

From Beckindale to Emmerdale

*As a peaceful outpost of rural England, Beckindale took a long
time to catch up with the 20th century. However, its tranquillity
was shattered by a plane crash that killed villagers as well as
those on board, ensuring that life could never be the same again
for those who survived and ushering in a change of name to
Emmerdale as the villagers struggled to face the future.*

Beckindale, in the Yorkshire Dales, was the archetypal feudal village, embracing the Norman system that William the Conqueror brought to England from France in the early Middle Ages, following his defeat of King Harold. Like many other English villages, it had a lord of the manor whose estate formed the focal point of the village and labourers who toiled on the land and joined the squire in the church every Sunday. They congregated at the parish church of St Mary's, which dates back to the 10th century, before the Norman invasion, and has been the scene of some memorable weddings and christenings, as well as the last resting place of many villagers.

For hundreds of years, farming was the main source of employment for a mostly static population. The work was hard and unrewarding, although no one is sure whether this tiny outpost knew anything of 19th-century agricultural workers' attempts to form a trade union, which led to the march of the six Tolpuddle Martyrs, in chains, from Dorset to Dorchester in 1834 and their transportation to Tasmania.

In fact, the 3,217 acres of Beckindale – 39 miles from Bradford and 52 miles from Leeds – seemed untouched by the outside world. Bronze Age artefacts and Roman remains testify that people settled there thousands of years ago, but most of the buildings date from the 18th and 19th centuries. The stream that flows through the village – the beck in the dale – gave rise to its name.

The Miffield estate was the biggest employer in the village, whose population was small until the middle of the 20th century. Lord Miffield gave the lease of Emmerdale Farm, on the edge of the village, to the Sugden family in the 1850s as a token of his gratitude after Josh Sugden had sacrificed his life for the Earl's son in the Crimean War. In the mid-20th century, Josh's great-grandson, Jacob Sugden, married Annie Pearson and continued as a tenant farmer there while her father, Sam, was employed as a labourer on the Miffield estate, then owned by George Verney. By 1972, when Jacob died, the farm was ailing, largely a result of the old man spending much of his last years in The Woolpack pub.

The village also boasted another pub, The Malt Shovel, a post office and stores, a village institute and – until its closure in the mid-1970s – a primary school. When Zoë Tate set up a veterinary practice in 1994, it was the first in Emmerdale since the days of John Stokes, Martin Butler and Margaret Beckett.

The nearest neighbouring villages are Connelton (2¾ miles away, with a primary school, shops, a library and the Feathers hotel and restaurant) and Robblesfield (3 miles in the opposite direction).

The market town of Hotten is 7½ miles from the village, which boasts excellent walks – such as that through Sparrow Wood – a river that wends its way through the dale and a hill called the Struggle that offers breathtaking views as far as Hotten and even Bradford.

Traditions Threatened

'Progress' was slow to find its way to Beckindale in the last quarter of the 20th century. It seemed that, when it did, many of the country traditions that had survived for centuries were threatened. The church fête was always an important event in the social calendar, and stalwarts such as Annie Sugden put enthusiasm into arranging the stalls. But, once the village lost its own vicar – as so many small communities have in recent decades – the fête disappeared and the vicarage garden, which played host to it, became overgrown.

As Beckindale is a farming village, the Seedcut and Harvest Supper were important events that marked the passing of the seasons. The Seedcut, which traditionally took place on the farm that was last to gather in its harvest, was a ritual whereby a corner of that farm's final field was left uncut for the spirit of the harvest to retreat into. The reigning Seeding King gave each young man of the village an ear of corn from the last sheaf. The owner of the one with the most seeds was chased by everyone in a race to the village hall, where all the community's unwed young women were waiting, one of them elected the Seedcut Queen. If the young man could reach her, he became the new Seeding King.

The Beckstone Thrash, a beating of the bounds, is one of many traditions upheld by Annie Sugden's father, Sam Pearson, until his death in 1984.

A week after the Seedcut, the Harvest Supper took place in the village hall, although in Annie's younger days it was held in a big barn. It was originally instituted as the farmers' way of thanking labourers for their work during the previous year. Pies, breads and cakes were produced by the farmers' wives, who also supplied the hams. The hall would be decorated with lanterns and bales of straw and, during his final years in the village, local squire George Verney contributed the traditional gift of a barrel of ale.

An important ritual that took place on the night of the Harvest Supper was a beating of the bounds known as the Beckstone Thrash, a harvest-time ritual going back to pagan times. At sunset, everyone gathered outside the closed doors of the village hall and waited for the Thrash to appear. The old men of the village then came into view as they marched around the parish boundary, each with a wooden staff tapping on the ground in one hand and a candle in the other, the aim being to 'thrash out' evil spirits. They were led by a village elder, carrying a very old staff.

Until his death in 1984, Annie's father, Sam Pearson, was owner of this staff. Boys of the village would join the end of this procession. Back inside the hall, a dance-band from Hotten led the entertainment, and the singing and dancing continued into the early hours. Of necessity, the farmworkers were given the following day off.

Sheepdog trials were an annual event in the Beckindale calendar, taking place every January, but they have now disappeared. However, a village bonfire is still held on Guy Fawkes' Night and, at Christmas, the forecourt of The Woolpack pub remains a place where carol singers can bring festive cheer.

The Woolpack has also been the venue for the Demdale Hunt to stop for a stirrup cup during their Boxing Day meet. Home Farm is the traditional venue for the Hunt Ball every March. In 1994, teenager Jessica McAllister – who had arrived from London the previous year – tried to sabotage the hunt, with which her mother, Angharad, had started to ride.

Another age-old village event is the annual cricket match between Emmerdale and neighbouring Robblesfield, dating back to 1903, with both teams playing to win the Butterworth Ball.

Show of Unity

The annual show proved a poignant affair in 1984 when Sam Pearson won first prize with his pumpkin, before dying in his sleep that night and depriving Beckindale of its primary keeper of traditions and folklore.

Sam, who had been chairman of the cricket club and on the committe of the bowls club, was also active in the horticultural society. Fortunately, he was not around in 1993 to see the Great Beckindale Marrow Contest, won by Home Farm gardener Nick Bates against seasoned horticulturalists Seth Armstrong and Amos Brearly. Amos's entry failed to reach the judges after young Scott Windsor stamped on it. It was an act that encapsulated the threat that this Dales village faced to its customs of old.

A similar occurrence put paid to the entire community's hopes of winning a Best Kept Village competition in 1983, when a rival dumped a cartload of horse manure in the forecourt of The Woolpack. More happily, the entire village enjoyed a street party to celebrate the Queen's Silver Jubilee on a sunny day in July 1977.

Politics rarely touches on the lives of villagers, but parish council elections are always keenly contested. In 1985, Seth challenged his NY Estates employer Alan Turner for a seat but lost by a narrow margin. Four years later, Alan went on to be elected to the district council, against competition from Kate Sugden, a newcomer to the village who had married Joe Sugden just a month earlier.

Beckindale's street party to celebrate the Queen's Silver Jubilee, in 1977, is a time for the whole village to join together in happiness.

Pulling Together

The normal petty differences found in any village community were largely put aside when, in 1987, Beckindale was threatened by government plans to test nearby Pencross Fell as a site for an underground nuclear waste dump, using mine shafts in the hills.

Indeed, when it became known that NY Estates had been aware of the proposals before they were revealed in the *Hotten Courier*, there was the threat of disunity between Joe Sugden, who was the company's regional manager, and his brother Jack, who had committed himself to the family farm after his return from Italy seven years earlier. Jack had also recently become a father and was showing increasing concern for his environment.

Joe's mother, Annie, told him that she did not want the Sugdens divided over the issue and he promised to attend a crisis public meeting that was called at the village hall. At the meeting, nuclear industry representative Mr Bailey was told in no uncertain terms that the community was united against the plans, with Archie Brooks and Jack leading the rebellion.

Although local MP Harriet Ridgley-Jones urged villagers to let the tests go ahead before making up their minds, and added that she would not vote against the proposals in Parliament, the Revd Donald Hinton made it clear that Beckindale would not accept even the smallest risk.

A second public meeting, in The Woolpack, saw the rift between Jack and Joe manifest itself in the way that their mother had hoped to avoid. Jack made a rallying call to fight 'the enemies of our community' and Joe responded with the view that nuclear power had arrived and the waste had to be dumped somewhere. 'I can't just turn my back on the real world and put up a barricade,' he said.

But Jack won the day, with villagers voting to mount an active campaign against the government's plans, and playgroup helper Dolly Skilbeck marshalling mothers to fight for the future of their children.

The following day, Mr Bailey arrived at the village hall for another meeting, to be confronted by placards that read 'Say No to a Shallow Grave' and

When a plane crashes over Beckindale in 1993, Archie Brooks is the first victim as a fireball crashes down from the sky.

'Beckindale Says No to Radioactive Waste'. Inside the hall, Archie Brooks – in a skeleton suit – emerged through clouds of smoke from a coffin daubed with nuclear symbols. Amid cheers and laughter, Mr Bailey abandoned the meeting, realising that the time was finished for talking.

As contractors set to work on the proposed dump site, villagers flocked there to protest. An angry exchange with Sgt MacArthur resulted in two arrests, but the work was successfully disrupted. The following day, locals pulled out all the stops to prevent the contractors' vehicles getting through. Jack's tractor and Matt Skilbeck's sheep blocked two roads to the site, while Jock McDonald dropped manure from a tipper trailer onto traffic that tried to use another route. However, the vehicles finally made their way through.

War had been declared. As the campaign continued, Matt was issued with a court injunction to stay away from the fell and Jack was arrested and served seven days in Armley Prison for contempt of court. While languishing there, he heard that the protest had been successful and plans for the dump abandoned. The village's greatest fight had been won – but an event that could not be foreseen or prevented was yet to come.

A New Dawn

Sleepy Beckindale was shaken to its foundations in 1993 by an event that ensured life would never be the same again for its inhabitants. On 30 December, Archie Brooks, Mark Hughes, Elizabeth Pollard, Leonard Kempinski and the Hutchinson family were killed when a plane carrying East European holidaymakers exploded over the village.

Such disasters had previously been seen by the people of Beckindale only on the television news. All those aboard the plane were killed instantly, débris was littered around Beckindale's green and pleasant land, gas mains exploded, bridges were destroyed and power supplies were cut off.

Hours earlier, a Dickensian Evening had begun at The Woolpack. When landlord Alan Turner – appropriately dressed as Mr Pickwick – banished Seth Armstrong from it, the rascally gamekeeper left the premises and threatened to take his custom to The Malt Shovel. Principled as ever, Archie Brooks walked out in protest. As his friend Nick Bates followed him, the first fireball came crashing down from the sky and scored a direct hit on Archie. His body was never recovered.

At the same time, leaving Nick's cottage in Demdyke Row, where she was babysitting granddaughter Alice, proved to be a fatal mistake for

Elizabeth Pollard. She stormed out following a row with husband Eric, threatening to expose a cheque fraud he had committed. She was never seen alive again. Concern about baby Alice was alleviated only the following morning, when her cries were heard as she miraculously lay alive under the rubble of the house.

The jollities at The Woolpack stopped as an explosion shattered the pub's windows and destroyed its wine bar. Meanwhile, at Whiteley's Farm, Lynn Whiteley escaped from the building with baby son Peter before it was engulfed in flames. But Mark Hughes, sent there by stepfather Joe to return a borrowed vacuum cleaner, did not come out alive. Such was the devastation that he was later identified only by a watch that Annie Sugden had given him – the one that she had presented to her first husband, Jacob, on their wedding day.

Joe had just started driving mother Annie and her new husband, Leonard Kempinski, to Leeds Bradford Airport for a holiday in Spain when a wing piece from the plane fell out of the sky and Joe swerved, causing the car to leave the road. Leonard was killed and Annie remained in a coma for three months.

Frank Tate and Jack Sugden proved to be the heroes of Beckindale's darkest hour. Frank was driving to visit estranged wife Kim at her new

A wing piece descends from the sky, causing Joe Sugden to swerve in an accident that leaves him on crutches, stepfather Leonard Kempinski dead and mother Annie in a coma.

Left Frank Tate drags estranged wife Kim from her blazing stables as she tries to save her beloved horses.

Above When a broken-down lorry blocks the bridge, Jack Sugden and Frank Tate work out a way of creating access for the emergency services.

stables to offer a peace-making belated Christmas present. When he arrived, the stables were ablaze. With Vic Windsor, the pair tried to fight the flames, but they eventually had to admit defeat as Frank dragged Kim away while she frantically tried to rescue her horses.

Then, with Jack, Frank masterminded a plan to clear the way for the emergency services. A broken-down lorry was blocking the bridge across the river, so they built a second one. Frank spotted pipes left by the construction company carrying out new drainage. Jack jumped into his tractor and, with Frank's supervision, lifted the pipes and placed them across the river to form a platform strong enough for ambulances and fire engines to cross.

Back at The Woolpack, where new local GP Bernard McAllister tended the injured, Alan Turner was gravely concerned about the fate of Seth, whose dog, Smokey, and cottage in Demdyke Row had been destroyed. Turner, a tough employer who deep down cared about Seth's welfare, was close to tears as Seth eventually reappeared with Samson the horse and the news that he had found refuge with widow Betty Eagleton, an old flame from the Second World War.

Samson proved another hero of the hour after Frank Tate's son, Chris, was dragged from the rubble of the wine bar. The horse helped to lift débris off Chris's legs and, although the disaster left him paralysed and confined to a wheelchair, the millionaire's son at least escaped with his life.

The rescue operation continued through the night. When morning came, the villagers had to face the cold light of day and confront the tragedy that had been visited upon them. Jack Sugden found dead animals strewn across his land and fields laid to waste by the chemicals and spillages.

There was no quick-fix solution. The families of those who died had to come to terms with their loss: Nick Bates was temporarily blinded and so

traumatised that he had to be hospitalised, Frank and Kim Tate were reunited and Kathy Tate abandoned plans to run away with wine salesman Josh Lewis so that she could look after husband Chris.

An official inquest into the disaster concluded that the plane had crashed as a result of structural weakness and recorded a verdict of accidental death on all the victims. As the villagers slowly began to rebuild their lives, Beckindale was renamed Emmerdale in an attempt to mark a new beginning and as a tribute to the Sugden family, who had done so much for the community over the years. Everyone has put the disaster behind them, but that night and its effect on a Dales village will never be forgotten.

Villagers mourn the loss of family and friends as Archie Brooks, Mark Hughes, Elizabeth Pollard and Leonard Kempinski are buried.

The 1993 plane crash brought *Emmerdale* its most dramatic moment – at a cost of £1 million. Filming took place over three weeks and special-effects designer Ian Rowley created some explosive action.

Esholt, where outdoor village scenes were then shot, looked as if it really had been victim to a disaster, with débris everywhere, fallen telegraph posts and overturned cars. Fire rigs were attached to different buildings, with the owners' permission, and prop telegraph poles were brought in and 'dressed' into the shots to appear real.

A special set was constructed at Rudding Park – the location used for Home Farm's Holiday Village – to show Kim Tate's stables alight after suffering a direct hit by a fireball. This provided greater space than the location at Sicklinghall previously used for the stables, giving more flexibility of camera movement. But a real-life disaster happened just before filming was due to take place.

'When the straw was being dressed into the set before the special effects were rigged, a cigarette end or something set it on fire,' says production controller Tim Fee. 'One of the worst fires to put out is straw. So filming stopped for the night and we then had to rake all the straw out of the barn. We set everything up again the next day and it went perfectly. A giant fireball covered in petrol was attached to a rope and placed on a 150ft-high crane. Then it was swung into the stables set, which also contained Kim's caravan, rigged with explosives, and everything was engulfed in flames.'

The scene of The Woolpack interior being hit by another fireball was shot on the studio set. A replica jukebox and sugar-glass glasses replaced the originals to ensure that there was no permanent damage. Stunt co-ordinator Stuart St Paul and a stuntman were seen drinking next to the jukebox before they – and it – were thrown over by the blast.

For the first time, an exterior of the pub's wine bar was built on to the back of the real pub in Esholt for scenes of Chris Tate being rescued from the rubble.

Roads near the Home Farm location, Creskeld Hall, were used for the scene of Joe Sugden's car leaving the road as a piece of aircraft wing fell from the sky – in reality dropped into shot by a crane again.

Filming of the plane crash scene, with débris littered around, was done at Rudding Park on an area where a swathe had been cut in the trees for the building of a golf course.

The hills around the viaduct near Esholt were used for filming the scene of Archie Brooks's death and Nick Bates being blinded. The spot of Archie's tragedy has become known as 'Archie's Hill'.

Emmerdale Farm

Farmhouse 1

1972–93	Annie Sugden, Jack Sugden (1972–3, 1980–2, 1988–9), Joe Sugden (1972–4, 1988–9, 1990–2), Sandie Merrick (1982–6), Jackie Merrick (1982–8), Robert Sugden (1988–9), Rachel Hughes (1989–90), Mark Hughes (1989–92), Jack Sugden and Sarah Connolly, Robert Sugden (all 1992–3)
Lodgers:	Dryden Hogben (1974), Christine Sharp (1974), James Bonfils (1974), Ray and Sarah (1977), Angela Read (1977), Dolly Acaster (1977), Amos Brearly (1978)

Attic

1972–3	Matt and Peggy Skilbeck
1973	Henry Wilks
1974	Joe Sugden
1974–80	Matt and Dolly Skilbeck (1978–80)
1982–8	Jack Sugden, Pat Merrick (later Sugden) (1982–6), Robert Sugden (1986–8)
1988	Jackie and Kathy Merrick
1989–90	Joe Sugden and Kate Hughes (later Sugden)
1990–2	Rachel Hughes

Front Parlour

1989	Revd Donald Hinton
1991	Henry Wilks

Farmhouse Extension

1980–9	Matt and Dolly Skilbeck, Sam Skilbeck (1982–89)
1989–92	Jack Sugden and Sarah Connolly (1990–2), Robert Sugden
1992–3	Rachel Hughes, Mark Hughes, Michael Feldmann (1992)

Farmhouse 2
(See also *Locations Past: Hawthorn Cottage*, page 166)

1993–7	Jack and Sarah Sugden, Robert Sugden (1993–7), Victoria Sugden (1994–7), Rachel Tate (1996), Joseph Hughes (1996), Andy Hopwood (1996–7)
Lodgers:	Seth Armstrong, Betty Eagleton (1994–5)

Farmhouse 3
(Formerly Melby's Farm)

1997–	Jack and Sarah Sugden, Robert Sugden, Victoria Sugden, Andy Hopwood
Guests:	Emma Cairns (1998)

CREATING REALITY

Now on its third site in both the fiction and reality, the location for Emmerdale Farm is at Burden Head Farm, in Harewood, on the road leading away from the outdoor village set.

As the centre of most of the action in the serial's early days, Emmerdale Farm's exterior scenes were first filmed at Lindley Farm, between Harrogate and Otley. Following farmer Arthur Peel's decision to retire, subsidence was written into the script in 1993 as a reason for the Sugden family moving to Hawthorn Cottage.

That house had previously existed in the story as the home of Matt and Peggy Skilbeck, then Joe Sugden. In 1993, Jack Sugden renamed it Emmerdale. That farm, at Eccup, was the same location on the Harewood estate that had originally been used in the 1970s.

Four years later, the farmhouse was bulldozed in the story to give access to a quarry and Jack and wife Sarah bought Woodside Farm. In reality, the move was engineered to improve a location with which the then producer, Mervyn Watson, and production designer Mike Long were not happy.

Carr House Cottages, on the Harewood estate, were used as the location for Woodside Farm (it was originally referred to as Carr House in the story, too). Mike had the derelict cottages converted when it was planned for Jack and Sarah Sugden to move in.

However, the couple never actually lived there. They stayed first in a caravan on the site, then in Tenant House, which belonged to Jack's mother, Annie, before deciding that too much work was needed on the property. In 1997, it was sold to the Cairns family, who left the serial in 1998.

Instead, the Sugdens moved to Melby's Farm and again renamed it Emmerdale, when a further change of location positioned it conveniently for

filming on the Harewood estate, about 1½ miles from the new village set that was planned. Mike Long added a porch outside the front door of the house, which is occupied by a shepherd employed by a tenant farmer on the estate.

'When we were building a studio set, I needed something to stop us seeing a backcloth immediately outside, so I built that porch,' explains Mike. The new interior – a composite set with a farmhouse kitchen and hallway leading to a sitting room – was built at the *Emmerdale* Production Centre in March 1997. 'It was the last set to go into the studio,' says Mike. 'The only similarity with the location is the front door and the window. The rest was down to my imagination.

'I wanted the colours inside to be a bit dowdy. Jack and Sarah could only just afford to buy this farmhouse, so I wanted it to look as if it needed a bit of work doing to it. We bought a lot of interesting props to get a country feel to it, including an Aga that we can actually cook on, and we obtained all the china at markets in Skipton, Wensleydale and places like that.

'We don't normally have time to do that but, because we were buying for the Harewood set at the same time, we were able to combine a lot of prop buying. There is also a back wall that swings out so that we can put a camera in and film from behind it.

'The piano in the sitting room was once in Annie Sugden's front parlour in the original farmhouse set. The chair belonging to her father, Sam Pearson, is also there but has been re-covered. A picture of the original Emmerdale farmhouse hangs in this room.

'I wanted the staircase to be seen from the sitting room because there are children in the house and you can view them going up to their bedrooms or coming downstairs.'

Jack Sugden (centre) returns after the death of his father to join Matt and Peggy Skilbeck (left), grandfather Sam Pearson (centre), mother Annie and younger brother Joe.

Farmed by the Sugdens since Lord Miffield granted its lease to the family in the 1850s, Emmerdale Farm – whose name comes from emmer, a species of wheat that has always flourished in the dale – originally covered 320 acres.

A Friesian cattle herd provided an important source of income, and there were Swaledale and cross-bred Masham sheep, with 50 acres set aside for barley and 10 for kale, and hens and geese roaming the farmyard. The farm's area was added to when 50 acres of Hathersage Farm was bought in 1979 and a further 70 acres was willed to Matt Skilbeck in 1987, after a recluse bequeathed him neighbouring Crosgill.

But, back in 1972, Annie Sugden faced an uncertain future as her farmer husband Jacob died after years of draining Emmerdale Farm's depleted profits away at The Woolpack pub, leaving the work to his younger son, Joe, along with daughter Peggy and her husband, Matt Skilbeck.

Jacob's elder son, Jack, had left the Dales farm for London eight years earlier at the age of 18 after rowing with his father about intensive farming. Instead of following tradition and waiting until the day came when he would take over the farm, Jack found fame and fortune as a writer, gaining acclaim for his novel *The Field of Tares*.

Voice From Beyond the Grave

But the wily old man, even after his death, aimed to change that. In his will, he left the running of the farm to Jack. This immediately fuelled bitterness and resentment in Joe, who felt aggrieved at not being rewarded for the toil and sweat he had put into the farm, and in Peggy, who already had a vision of breaking away from it eventually and living in suburbia with Matt by selling her share.

So Jack returned to the farm and village of his childhood, making his appearance at the funeral tea after watching from a distance as his father was buried on 16 October 1972, six days after his death from pneumonia.

Unenthusiastically, he went back to living and working with his family, then saw the potential for converting a derelict watermill on Emmerdale land, believing it would give him the right environment for writing a second novel. A friend from London, Bart Ansett, arrived to help Jack with the work.

Clash of the Titans

As one man returned to the village of his birth, another arrived for the first time after a successful career as a Bradford wool merchant. Henry Wilks moved to Beckindale to take early retirement following the death of his wife. He took up residence at Inglebrook, a short distance away from the farm, with his daughter, Marian.

When the Sugdens first encountered Henry, the meeting was acrimonious. The bluff businessman wanted to exercise his right to use an ancient right of way across Emmerdale land, which had long been forgotten.

Steeling himself for a battle, Henry briefed his solicitor, Mr Peters, in Hotten, but Jack proved a match for him by discovering that the disputed carriageway followed an even older path, buried in mud over the years, that continued beyond the farm into Inglebrook land, past Henry's drawing-room window. That was the end of the matter.

Henry Wins the War

Jack won the first battle, but Henry was to win the war after a 30-acre plot of land known as Jameson's, between Inglebrook and the watermill land, was put up for sale when farmer Harry Jameson decided to move away.

Competing with Jack to buy the land, Henry discovered that the Sugdens did not own the freehold of their land and it was up for sale. He ended up buying both Jameson's Farm and Emmerdale Farm land, which made him the Sugdens' new landlord.

A Peace Pact

Henry had no intention of making life difficult for the Sugden family. In fact, as he sat down in Annie's kitchen for the first time in January 1973, he put forward a proposal that would benefit himself as a businessman and them as farmers. He was also aware that Jack was falling for his daughter,

Marian, and believed this might secure her future.

Looking to provide firm foundations for the farm's future, Henry suggested that they should turn it into a limited company. He would invest in capital to buy stock and replace worn-out equipment. At the same time, shares would be distributed between him, Annie, Jack, Joe, Peggy and Annie's father, Sam Pearson, who was retired after a lifetime working on the Verney family's estate, latterly as farm manager.

Jack refused to take part in the business and passed his shares on to the others in the family. Sam did not want shares in Emmerdale Farm Ltd and took a cash payment of £500 instead, using the money to buy a new suit and a puppy, Bess. Peggy's husband, Matt, was not offered a share but was to receive a wage to continue as a labourer, as Joe did.

This settlement secured the future of the farm, Peggy became secretary of the limited company and Joe and Matt set about restocking and building up the milk herd.

Jack Isolated

Although Jack did not want to return to the fold, he helped out at the farm occasionally and later found himself in conflict with Henry over plans to build a pig unit. That was one instance when Henry eventually had to admit defeat.

Jack had by then given up ideas of completing the conversion work at The Mill and moved into the building as it was in January 1973. His relationship with Marian Wilks fizzled out and she left that month to see the world, taking a Greek islands cruise and ending up in New Zealand, before eventually settling in Italy.

Laughter and Tears

Matt and Peggy were on the move, too, after the birth of their twins, Sam and Sally, on 10 April 1973. Following agreement at a board meeting, they switched from the farmhouse attic to Jameson's Farm, which Henry had previously earmarked for developing as holiday cottages. They renamed it Hawthorn Cottage and started family life there.

However, tragedy struck just three months after the twins' birth when, on 16 July, Peggy died suddenly of a subarachnoid haemorrhage (a blood vessel bursting in the brain). The Revd Ruskin proved a great source of comfort for the family as they grieved for Peggy, who was buried next to her father in the churchyard.

When the twins were subsequently christened at St Mary's Church, two of the godparents were newcomers to the village – Alison Gibbons, who had come from Liverpool to work at the shop following the death of her husband and young child, and Henry Wilks, who had become a great friend to the Sugdens in such a short time.

Henry stayed in the attic at the farm for a short time after his cottage was razed in a fire. Then he moved to The Woolpack and, shortly afterwards, became Amos Brearly's business partner in the pub. After Annie Sugden injured her wrist, the twins went to live with Matt's Aunt Beattie, who had once been a children's nanny, and her husband, Ben, in Blackfell, three miles away.

Matt was one of several villagers who enjoyed the company of Alison Gibbons, and she could have been a good mother to Sam

Twins Sam and Sally have no shortage of love from their father Matt, grandmother Annie and Henry Wilks after their mother's death.

and Sally. But eventually Matt and Alison parted, realising that they had been brought together only by their similar circumstances.

In the wake of Peggy's death, Matt turned inward and ploughed himself into his work. He was rewarded when, in 1974, his ewes won first prize at the Great Yorkshire Show, in Harrogate.

Just the Job

Another newcomer to arrive at the farm – shortly after Jack left Beckindale and The Mill to work on a film script of his novel in Rome – was traveller Dryden Hogben, who turned up in the yard one morning asking for a bucket of water. He had started camping on Emmerdale land, which he claimed was his right.

When the Sugdens discovered that Dry, as he liked to be called, was a good handyman, they employed him to do odd jobs and then to convert the farmhouse attic into a bedroom for Joe, simply by installing some floorboards and a new window. He was adamant that he would not alter the beams, even though one was so low that people had to watch their heads.

Joe had previously shared a room with his grand-father, Sam, but his new duty in doing the accounts since Peggy's death meant that he often stayed up late. Dry then joined Joe in painting the farmhouse kitchen.

But Dry suddenly fled to Ireland when a woman called Celia arrived at The Woolpack looking for him. Apparently, she had been his fiancée and he had jilted her at the altar.

Joe's Unhappy Marriage

Joe did not have much time to make use of the attic room because, on 10 September 1974, he married Milk Marketing Board official Christine Sharp and moved into Hawthorn Cottage, with Matt switching to the attic at Emmerdale.

Sportscar-driving Christine had arrived at the farm after Joe decided that it should become accredited. This meant that its milk herd had to be tested over a period of time and certified brucellosis-free. Accredited cows would earn Emmerdale more

Joe's marriage to Christine Sharp is doomed from the start when her wealthy father disapproves, and the fun-loving woman walks out on her husband after five weeks.

money from the Milk Marketing Board and bullocks would fetch more at market.

Joe fell for Christine, who then gave up her job and persuaded the Sugdens to let her live at the farm because she claimed that her rented cottage was no longer available, although this proved to be untrue.

One day, her father – a wealthy businessman who ran a dairy farm as a hobby – arrived at Emmerdale, ordered Christine to go home at once and was appalled to learn of her engagement to Joe. But she insisted on staying, bought a beautiful wedding dress in Harrogate, and a date was fixed for the wedding.

The ceremony took place, with the men wearing morning suits, Henry Wilks giving Christine away – when her father, Robert, refused to attend – and Matt acting as best man. Although Joe sent a telegram to Jack in Rome, his elder brother failed to attend the wedding. Shortly afterwards, Jack invited his mother to Rome for two weeks to see him receive an Italian prize for his first novel. Her father, Sam, who had recently suffered a slight stroke, joined Annie on the trip.

Joe and Christine honeymooned in London and returned to Beckindale, where Christine set about transforming Hawthorn Cottage into a comfortable home. But her spending, on items such as expensive antique furniture from an upmarket Harrogate shop, worried Joe, who had led a simple life.

Annie returned from Italy to discover that Christine had walked out on Joe after only five weeks of marriage, following a row about money. He had found out that the furniture had been charged to her father's account and she thought they could pay him back when they could afford it. When he ordered her to send it back, she refused and left.

Eventually, Joe found Christine staying at the museum where her former boyfriend worked. She insisted she would not return to him and, a few days later, returned her engagement ring. Although the couple attempted a reconciliation in 1976, it failed and a divorce went ahead that year.

Lodger's Lesson

At around the time of Matt's win at the Great Yorkshire Show, new village schoolteacher James Bonfils arrived in Beckindale. He was due to rent Beryl Crossthwaite's cottage, but she had not let Annie know, so it was not aired and the furniture had not arrived. As a result, Annie offered him temporary accommodation at the farmhouse.

An English Rose

One communication that did get through was a letter to Annie from Jean Kendall, her cousin in Middlesbrough, who wrote that she was ill and did not have much money. She was particularly worried about her 16-year-old daughter, Rosemary, who had recently left school.

Annie sent Jean the money from her birthday calf – a country custom whereby the first calf born after midnight on your birthday becomes your property – which annoyed her father, Sam, because Annie had earmarked it to fund a car after starting driving lessons and the Sugdens had not spoken to the Kendalls for years after a family feud.

Then, when Jean collapsed and was admitted to hospital, Annie took in Rosemary. A kind, considerate teenager, she soon became a favourite of Sam and proved a great asset in helping to run the farm when Annie became a churchwarden and took driving lessons. On her seventeenth birthday the old man presented Rosemary with a birthday

calf, but she was heartbroken to discover that it would one day be sold for beef.

City girl Rosemary developed a crush on Joe and, perhaps partly because of her interest in him, grew to love animals. But Joe was unaware of her interest and in 1976 she started seeing Jim and Freda Gimbel's son, Martin, who was 20 but was expected to work on his father's farm for a pittance.

Although Martin's mother wanted him to become engaged to Rosemary, he did not want to do so. He continually rowed with his overbearing and anti-social father. Then, after a final argument, he walked out and joined the Army. Rosemary eventually returned to her mother in Middlesbrough.

Matt Devastated

On 13 January 1976, Matt, who had lost his wife three years earlier, was devastated to hear that his children, Sam and Sally, had been killed in a road accident together with his Aunt Beattie, when a train hit her car after it stalled on a level crossing.

He learned of the disaster when a policeman flagged down his car on the Hotten road, and he spent the night stumbling around on the moors in his anguish. Burying himself in his work once more, Matt – an orphan himself – inherited Peggy's share of the farm.

In the autumn, Jack returned from Rome for a short visit so that he could see his London publisher to discuss his second novel, which he was having difficulty in writing.

Meanwhile, Sam decided he was not too old to marry again and proposed to old flame Nellie Ratcliffe. She turned him down, but he still led a campaign to stop NY Estates evicting Nellie from her cottage.

A Doomed Affair

Jim Gimbel's daughter, Kathy, socialised with Joe, with whom she had been at school, and with teacher James Bonfils. She had married local bad boy Terry Davis after getting pregnant but then miscarried, left him and returned to her family at Holly Farm.

Joe began to get closer to Kathy and the pair began an affair that caused a scandal in Beckindale.

Tragic Matt appears to have found happiness with his marriage to Woolpack barmaid Dolly Acaster in 1978.

Both were waiting for their divorces but felt they could put their failed marriages behind them.

The relationship was put to the test when Christine returned in the autumn of 1976, looking for a reconciliation. Joe responded by filing for divorce. Christine's father tried to claim half of Joe's share in Emmerdale Farm as part of the settlement, but Henry Wilks advised Joe to threaten Robert Sharp with a counter-claim on half of his dairy farm. That was the end of the matter and divorce proceedings went ahead.

In 1977 Joe sold Hawthorn Cottage and bought 3 Demdyke Row, moving in with Kathy. But the affair ended when Kathy could no longer cope with the pressure of her own family disowning her and the village gossip.

The final straw was her father killing himself with his own shotgun after wife Freda walked out on him as a result of his raising a hand to their younger son, Davy. Racked with guilt, Kathy left for Hotten and Joe was heartbroken again.

Matt Wins Dolly

The farmhouse became a refuge for a number of people during 1977. An unemployed man called Ray and his heavily pregnant wife, Sarah, stayed there after their cottage was devastated when lightning caused a tree to fall on it. Another guest was problem teenager Angela Read, who came from a broken home and stayed with the Sugdens as part of a church-sponsored scheme.

A more significant arrival was that of new Woolpack barmaid Dolly Acaster, who came to help out after Annie broke her wrist. After Matt dumped short-term girlfriend Lucy Stubbs, a trainee agricultural advisory officer at Hotten Market with the Agricultural Development and Advisory Service, he fell for Dolly.

Their future was threatened when, the following year, Dolly's former boyfriend, Richard Roper, arrived. She harboured the secret that he was the father of her illegitimate son, who had been given up for adoption. At the time, Richard had been persuaded by his domineering mother to flee to South Africa, but he now hoped to win Dolly back.

He said he had hired private detectives to find her and he also wanted to trace their son so that they could settle down as a family. Dolly was torn between Richard and Matt, not sure of her new lover's intentions.

She arranged to meet Richard at a country hotel, where she told him that they had no future together. Tipped off about the meeting by pub landlord Amos Brearly, Matt arrived at the hotel and persuaded Dolly to stay in Beckindale.

Despite attempts by Dolly's mother, Phyllis Acaster, to prevent her daughter marrying Matt, the wedding went ahead at St Mary's Church on 29 June 1978, with Amos giving his barmaid away. The couple moved into the farmhouse together, but they were able to live more independently when a barn was converted into a two-bedroom cottage extension in 1980.

Annie Saves the Day

Annie's quick thinking saved a potentially life-threatening situation when, in 1978, teenagers Steve Hawker and Pip Coulter arrived at the farm and held Sam at gunpoint after robbing The Woolpack. She provided them with a car so that they could escape and there was no violence.

Sam was proud when Italy-based grandson Jack had his second novel, *One Man in Time*, published – based on his grandfather's life. Memories also flooded back for Annie when David Annersley arrived in Beckindale. She had had a crush on him during the early days of her marriage to Jacob but remained faithful to her husband. An unexpected guest at the farm in 1978 was Woolpack landlord Amos Brearly, who contracted chickenpox from Seth Armstrong's son, Fred, and moved out of the pub to recuperate.

When NY Estates bought the Miffield estate from the Verney family during the same year, it emerged that the farm's 20-acre meadow, known as Top Twenty, did not belong to the Sugdens. Jacob had simply rented it for a bottle of whisky a year – a payment known as the 'Verney Bottle'. A dispute ended with the Sugdens agreeing to buy the land.

Threats and Plans

Local bad boy Phil Fletcher, who owed money to Emmerdale Farm, accused Joe of deliberately shooting him in the leg during an argument over game shooting rights on the Sugdens' land in 1979. In an attempt to make the charge stick, Fletcher forced his son, Terry, to lie to the police, but they believed neither father nor son.

Henry and Sam's long-time dream of opening a farm museum appeared as if it might be fulfilled when Ed Hathersage and land agent Geoff Atwill unveiled plans for one on land next to the farm. However, the project eventually fell through.

Jack In, Joe Out

Major changes took place at the farm in 1980 following Jack's return from Italy. He was finally to put his writing life behind him and concentrate on making a success of the family farm that his father had intended to be his eight years earlier.

It seemed an appropriate moment for younger brother Joe to reappraise his working life and, after a trip to America, he jumped at the opportunity to become assistant manager at Home Farm after Richard Anstey became NY Estates' boss there. Joe, who had always been interested in new agricultural developments, had become frustrated at Emmerdale and saw this job as a new challenge.

Jack and Pat Reunited

Jack's homecoming coincided with another return to the village – that of his teenage sweetheart Pat Harker. He had jilted her back in 1964, when he left the farm to go to London, unaware that she was pregnant. Pat had married Tom Merrick and let him believe that son Jackie was his child. The couple later had a daughter, Sandie.

Jack finally marries childhood sweetheart Pat Merrick at Hotten Register Office in 1982.

Pat had now walked out on Tom because of his violence and brought her children to Beckindale to start afresh. After staying with Pat's Aunt Elsie, they moved into a caravan and Pat took a job as a waitress at Hotten Market. The following year, she became the Revd Donald Hinton's housekeeper.

Tom, who had previously worked as a labourer on the farm, arrived back in Beckindale in 1981 after receiving a suspended sentence for stealing Christmas trees from NY Estates. He was determined to get back his estranged wife, who had rekindled the flames with Jack. When Pat petitioned for divorce, on the grounds of mental and physical abuse, Tom beat her up and, blaming Jack for her refusal to take him back, tried to implicate her new lover in an arson attack.

However, Jack and Pat's romance continued un-abated and, after a summer weekend away together in Scarborough, they decided to marry once Pat's divorce had come through. Jack's grandfather disapproved of him marrying a divorcée, but Sam's old flame Nellie Ratcliffe spoke up for Pat and her right to happiness.

Just before Christmas 1981, Pat's divorce was finalised and the wedding could be planned. However, the Sugden household – including Jack – was shocked by the revelation that Jackie was Jack's son.

Not a Good Year

Annie was also shocked earlier in the year when she was confronted by a burglar at the farm while recuperating from an operation on her leg. He ran off and was never caught. This was one of a number of attempted robberies in the village in 1981, when further bad news came as Jack's prize cattle herd contracted salmonella and had to be slaughtered.

Even more bad news came when Dolly heard that her mother, by then living in Switzerland with her second husband, Leonard Purwick, had suffered a brain haemorrhage. Fortunately, she survived.

As the farm gradually expanded its sheep capacity, following the failure of the farm museum, Matt and Jack bought a new sheep shelter from Clifford Longthorn, the tenant at Lower Hall Farm.

The following year, new NY Estates manager Alan Turner tried to poach Matt to become his assistant manager, offering him the late Enoch Tolly's farmhouse as an inducement, but Matt stayed loyal to Emmerdale and Joe continued in that position at Home Farm.

Jack Marries Pat

Hotten Register Office was the venue, on 5 October 1982, for Jack and Pat's wedding, with the bride wearing a fetching apricot outfit. The Revd Donald Hinton had refused to marry the couple in church because Pat was a divorcée.

Pat's son, Jackie, had found it difficult to come to terms with the fact that Jack was his natural father and resented him. At the same time, his real father disowned him. Turning to drink, Jackie left the farmhouse and returned to the dingy caravan that he and his family had previously rented from NY Estates. He was later given community service for burning down the caravan.

Dolly's Dream

Meanwhile, four years after their wedding, a dream came true for Dolly and Matt, who had longed for a baby. Dolly had happily announced her pregnancy in 1979 but miscarried after eight months and almost lost her life during the ordeal. In an attempt to overcome her depression, she became a helper with the local playgroup and, in 1981, its leader.

Early the following year, as Dolly experienced problems in conceiving again, she visited a specialist to discuss the matter. Shortly afterwards, she became pregnant and made a dramatic dash to hospital on 23 December 1982 when she suddenly went into labour and called on Jackie Merrick to drive her there, even though he had no licence.

Christened at St Mary's Church, the baby was to have been called David Samuel, but Matt's grandfather, Sam, thought they were naming the boy after him, so the couple switched the names around to avoid upsetting him.

Uncertainties Abound

After Jack and Pat's wedding and Dolly giving birth to Sam in 1982, the following year proved to be one of uncertainties for the Sugdens. Finances were tight at the farm, so Annie insisted that Henry Wilks take charge of the accounts.

Meanwhile, Joe left Beckindale for an NY Estates job in France, following the break-up of his affair with the Revd Donald Hinton's married daughter, Barbara Peters. Shortly after Joe's departure, in October, Annie was rushed to hospital and diagnosed as having peritonitis.

Then Pat's daughter, Sandie, revealed that she was pregnant but refused to name the father. She found support from Dolly, who still harboured the secret that she had an illegitimate child herself. It turned out that the father was studious Hotten Comprehensive sixth-former Andy Longthorn, son of farmer Clifford. He had slept with Sandie after plying her with sherry at the vicarage, where her brother, Jackie, was staying after committing the arson attack on his caravan.

Jackie gave Andy a black eye on discovering what had happened, but Andy's father insisted that his son would marry Sandie, give up his studies and take over Lower Hall Farm when he came of age. But Sandie had no wish to marry and Andy left for university.

Finding mother Pat unsympathetic, Sandie travelled to Aberdeen, where father Tom was based while working on the oil rigs. Baby daughter Louise was born there before Christmas and given up for adoption.

In the New Year, Sandie decided to start life afresh in Beckindale and returned with her father, Tom. Pat had not visited her daughter in Scotland, so there was tension between them. But Jack's grandfather, Sam, was instrumental in reconciling the teenager with her mother and Sandie took a job at Hotten Market.

Meanwhile, Tom Merrick was in trouble again, caught poaching fish with Derek Warner and Kevin Haynes by NY Estates gamekeeper Seth Armstrong. Son Jackie, who worked as assistant gamekeeper, blamed Seth for handing the gang over to the police.

Love Cheat Jack

Less than four years into their marriage, Jack cheated on Pat by having an affair with Hotten Market auctioneer's assistant Karen Moore. This followed the news that his former girlfriend, Marian Wilks, had married Paolo Rossetti in Italy.

When Pat discovered her husband's infidelity, she gave him an ultimatum – give up Karen or lose his wife. Jack returned to Pat and the Sugdens were united for Christmas, with Joe coming home on a short visit from France.

Sadly, one member of the family missing from the festive season was Sam Pearson, who died peacefully in his sleep on 27 November 1984. Annie discovered her father's body on taking him his morning cup of tea. The previous evening, Sam – a great upholder of country traditions – had been celebrating his first prize for a pumpkin he had entered in the village's annual show.

Jackie Nurses Wounds

After a broken romance with Alison Caswell, Jackie Merrick bought himself a motorcycle, only to be accidentally knocked down by NY Estates manager Alan Turner in his Range Rover on a dark country lane in 1985.

During a five-month stay in hospital, nursing broken bones, Jackie fell for nurse Sita Sharma and, after his return to the farmhouse at Emmerdale, the couple became engaged. However, Sita later called off their wedding plans, claiming that Jackie had pressurised her too much.

One good result of his long time in hospital was the time it gave Jackie to think about his life and future. He reconciled his differences with Jack and even called him 'Dad' for the first time.

Mowlem, Matt and Murder

Quarry owner Harry Mowlem, who joined forces with Derek Warner to rob a security van of £6000 in 1985, bought 30 acres of land adjoining Emmerdale Farm so that he could raise pigs. He also started making advances to Dolly, who miscarried again shortly afterwards.

When, the following January, Mowlem was violently murdered, the chief suspect was Dolly's husband, Matt. Shortly before his death, Matt had accused Mowlem of sheep stealing and attacked him in a violent rage.

Charged with manslaughter, Matt protested his innocence. But that was established only after £6000 from the security van robbery was found hidden in Mowlem's pig shelter. Derek Warner then held the Revd Donald Hinton hostage at the vicarage in a failed attempt to escape. On being captured by the police, he admitted that he had killed Mowlem after an argument about the stolen money.

A Son for Jack

Following Jack's affair of the previous year, he and Pat had a happier 1986, dominated by the birth of son Robert on 22 April. Joe was at the baby's christening the following month, having returned from France to become NY Estates regional manager.

But the reunited family was rocked by the death of Pat in a car accident on 26 August, just four months after Robert's birth. When she swerved to avoid a flock of sheep, the car left the road and plunged down a hillside, leaving Pat dead.

Friction at the Market

On his return, Joe moved back into his cottage in Demdyke Row. Jackie, who had been staying there, returned to the farmhouse because he did not get on with Joe. Shortly afterwards, he began a romance with Kathy Bates.

One of Joe's first decisions in his new job was for NY Estates to buy Hotten Market. He then caused friction in the Sugden family by dating Karen Moore, with whom Jack had conducted his affair, but the romance died.

When Karen left her job as auctioneer, Sandie Merrick took her place and found herself in conflict with new market manager Eric Pollard. Sandie herself caused a scandal by falling for married man Phil Pearce and moving out of the farmhouse and into The Mill.

Skeleton Out of the Cupboard

Just before Christmas 1986, Dolly's secret came back to haunt her when Graham Lodsworth, the illegitimate son whom she had given up for adoption almost 20 years earlier, arrived in Beckindale after a quest to find her.

He told her of his glamorous life in the Army but failed to add that he had deserted. Living rough in the woods, he set fire to his own car and, after he was detained by police in the New Year, a sergeant-major arrived to take him back to barracks.

Fire and Passion

Some of Jack's old fire returned in 1987 when he led a campaign to prevent the government siting a nuclear waste dump at nearby Pencross Fell, and when Henry Wilks's daughter, Marian, visited Beckindale with her husband Paolo and newborn son Niccolo, his heart was clearly where it had been 15 years earlier. While Paolo lay in a coma after preventing a burglary, Marian had a fling with Jack.

Jackie Weds Kathy

Jackie's stormy relationship with Kathy Bates was

threatened by the arrival in Beckindale of smooth-talking NY Estates trainee Tony Marchant. Jackie responded by vandalising Tony's van, making Kathy see his true feelings for her. But his misfortunes were added to when he fell down a mineshaft while trying to rescue a sheep. After surviving freezing conditions, he himself was rescued.

Kathy married Jackie in a church wedding on 3 February 1988 and, following a honeymoon in Tunisia, moved into the attic at Emmerdale Farm before moving into Joe's cottage in Demdyke Row in December. Kathy, working on the farm, contracted a rare virus from a sheep that caused her to miscarry. Worse was to follow when Jackie died in a shooting accident in August 1989.

Dolly's Escape Route

Matt was surprised to find out that an elderly recluse called Metcalfe, whom he had helped in the past, left him Crossgill Farm on his death in 1987. Matt hired Phil Pearce to renovate the farmhouse, but it was razed in May the following year when Phil carelessly left rags to burn in it. A further tragedy was averted when Annie, trapped inside, was rescued by Phil and Dolly.

For Dolly, Crossgill had represented a chance for her and Matt to live on their own, away from Emmerdale Farm, but Matt was privately relieved at the way things had turned out. The marriage was on the rocks and Dolly fell for timber consultant Stephen Fuller. They secretly went on holiday together, but she finally ended their on-off romance.

Dolly was shocked to hear, shortly afterwards, that Stephen had been killed by a falling tree and, blaming herself for his death, she took charge of funeral arrangements at Kelthwaite. By then, her marriage was all but over. She walked out on Matt early in 1989 and moved to The Mill with son Sam. Unable to come to terms with his broken marriage, Matt left Beckindale in November to become manager of a sheep farm near West Raynham, in Norfolk.

Annie experienced difficulties, too, coming to rely on tranquillisers after the trauma of her lucky escape. Kathy Merrick was the first to tackle her

Annie is rescued by Phil Pearce and Dolly Skilbeck when Crossgill, the farm inherited by Matt, goes up in flames.

about the problem, but it was Henry – Annie's most trusted confidant – who eventually persuaded her to flush the tablets down the toilet.

New Loves for Jack and Joe

Love was in the air during 1988. First, Jack started dating headstrong mobile librarian Sarah Connolly and it was not long before she moved in with him. But she did not want anything to do with farming and made Jack seal off the connecting door between the cottage extension they shared and the farmhouse, where Jack's mother, Annie, ruled the roost.

The couple's relationship was tested when Henry Wilks's daughter, Marian, visited Beckindale

*Teenager Rachel Hughes and married salesman Pete
Whiteley cause a scandal when they have an affair.*

hoping to rekindle her romance with Jack, but this time he resisted.

Brother Joe, who returned to work on the farm after a brief period managing the Home Farm estate in the wake of NY Estates' withdrawal from the village, found new love following his broken romance with vet Ruth Pennington. Divorcée Kate Hughes arrived in Beckindale with her teenage children, Rachel and Mark, and stayed at The Mill with Sandie Merrick.

In February 1989, after a short romance with Joe, she moved into the farmhouse at Emmerdale with him. The strained relationship he experienced with Mark gradually disappeared and, on 12 April, Joe married Kate at St Mary's Church, believing himself to have found the woman for whom he had so long been searching.

Weathering the Storm

Jack and Sarah's relationship was tested when Sarah's friend Gerry invited her on holiday to Portugal. She accepted the offer after a row with Jack, even though she had not intended to because she was fully committed to him and his son, Robert.

Then the affairs of Jack's former girlfriend Marian brought temptation his way again. When she was held by Italian police following the death of her husband, Jack flew out to see her and offer support. This made Sarah believe that he still loved Marian, but Jack returned and insisted that his future was with her.

Salesman's Techniques

There were long-term consequences for Joe's wife, Kate, when daughter Rachel had an affair with married salesman Pete Whiteley. He bedded the girl on her eighteenth birthday, in September 1989, but ended the relationship two months later. Rachel then confessed all to her mother.

Pete and his wife, Lynn, who lived with his father, Bill, at Whiteley's Farm, left the village for Birmingham but returned to Beckindale the following year. Pete resumed the affair and, after an argument with Rachel in The Woolpack in August, she stormed out and took his car keys to

prevent him driving while drunk. Kate then slapped Pete's face and ordered him to stay away from her daughter.

Shortly after Pete set off on foot in the dark, Kate – over the drink-drive limit – drove from the pub and accidentally ran him over. Two months later, Kate was sentenced to two years in prison after a court found her guilty of manslaughter.

On the day of her husband's funeral, Lynn Whiteley had given birth to their first child, son Peter Jr. Kate herself had become pregnant and miscarried in 1990, shortly before son Mark was caught shoplifting. Then, her ex-husband, David Hughes, had arrived in Beckindale in the hope of winning Kate back after leaving the Army. He even threatened Joe with a shotgun in the milking shed one morning, but Kate turned up and made David see sense.

However, she could not come to terms with what she had done. On her release from prison in 1991, Kate suffered a nervous breakdown, told Joe that she could never return to him and left to live with her father in Sheffield.

Joe remained bewildered about why his second marriage had bitten the dust but faced the task of looking after Kate's teenage children. By then, Rachel had become engaged to Michael Feldmann, who worked as a labourer at Emmerdale Farm, just before she set off for Leeds University and a three-year degree course.

Sarah Keeps Her Cool

When council budget cuts caused Sarah's mobile library job to be axed in 1990, she found new work pulling pints at The Woolpack. Then, in September, Jack proposed marriage and Sarah turned him down, but he pledged to make the same proposal every year on the anniversary of their first meeting.

Sarah had more worrying affairs on her mind the following year when, following Chris Tate's wedding to Kathy Merrick, she was kidnapped by Jim Latimer, who had just been released from jail after serving a sentence for the rape and murder of Sharon Crossthwaite back in 1973. He bore a grudge against Jack, who helped to convict him, and Sarah not only looked like Sharon but had the same initials. Fortunately, Sarah remained cool while being held in a disused building by Latimer and was eventually released unhurt.

She also kept her cool in 1992 when young widow Lynn Whiteley – who also lost her father-in-law, Bill, the previous year – tried to seduce Jack after luring him back to her farmhouse. Sarah humiliated Lynn in The Woolpack in front of a crowd that included her arch-enemy Rachel.

Lynn became reclusive after this incident, but her lodger, Archie Brooks, persuaded her to face villagers again and even Rachel adopted a more friendly manner towards her. Rachel also took a part-time job as a barmaid at the pub.

Joe Leaves Again

When Joe decided to leave the farm in 1992 to become manager of Frank Tate's newly opened Holiday Village, with accommodation in the Home Farm nursery flat, Jack and Sarah moved into the spacious farmhouse and Rachel and Mark switched to the cottage extension. With Joe gone, Michael Feldmann started working full-time on the farm.

Mark split up with girlfriend Melanie Clifford when he realised that he could not live up to her academic expectations for him. After forfeiting the chance to go to Glasgow University by failing his A-levels, Mark took a job as handyman at the Holiday Village and even shared a cabin with new girlfriend Lisa one night.

While Rachel was away at Leeds University, Mark took the opportunity to decorate the cottage to his taste – which included the colour purple – so she moved in fiancé Michael Feldmann to implement her taste and he replaced the gaudy purple with a light green.

However, the two lads were soon neglecting the housework and giving Jack and Sarah next door earache with their loud music. Events got out of hand when, one evening, Jack was assaulted outside the cottage by a couple of thugs who were attempting to gatecrash a party they believed to be going on there.

Rachel Dumps Michael

Meanwhile, Rachel was having doubts about her engagement to Michael and eventually handed back the engagement ring. But Michael refused to accept that their relationship was over. He went off the rails and, after Frank Tate refused him the tenancy of Winslow's Farm, joined the Rt Hon. Neil Kincaid's stablehand in a violent robbery at Home Farm in which Joe was beaten and left unconscious.

After being charged with burglary, Michael broke the conditions of his bail when he became obsessed with following Rachel and her new boyfriend, medical student Jayesh Parmar. Watching them in Beckindale one day in 1993, he saw Jack's son, Robert, fall into a river and saved the boy by jumping in, fully clothed.

As a result, Jack offered Michael his job back at Emmerdale Farm, but that was cut short when the hero was sentenced to four months in Roxleigh Prison for his part in the Home Farm robbery. Compensation came with letters and prison visits from Rachel, but the flames of romance were not rekindled.

On his release, there was no farm work available but Jayesh surprisingly managed to get Michael a job in a Leeds newsagent's. He found accommodation – and short-lived romance – at Whiteley's Farm with Lynn Whiteley.

Spanish Inquisition

Following Amos Brearly's retirement to Spain and the death of Henry Wilks in 1991, Annie took the opportunity to visit Amos for a winter break at his Spanish villa. On her return the following year, it became apparent that she had gained an admirer while there.

But – with Joe, Jack and Sarah trying to get information from Annie about her exploits in Spain – it was a long time before she revealed him to be Polish-born ex-serviceman Leonard Kempinski, an acquaintance of Amos.

Then, she shocked Jack and Joe by revealing that she was contemplating leaving and selling her share of the farm. This posed problems because the only capital was that left by Henry, and Jack felt that it should be held on to as a reserve, especially at a time of falling prices and bad returns. Mark helped out by working on the farm for little money for a while, but it was then left to Jack to work long hours, day after day.

So, when Leonard arrived in Beckindale just before Christmas 1992, he received a hostile reception from Annie's sons, with Jack accusing him of being out to get his mother's money. As a result, Leonard prepared to leave, but Amos informed Jack and Joe that his friend was a wealthy businessman. The brothers apologised to Leonard, who stayed and enjoyed the festivities at Emmerdale before flying off to Spain with Annie and Amos.

Farmhouse Move

Jack faced greater problems when, in 1993, it became clear that the farmhouse was suffering from subsidence, caused by old lead-mine workings. Early signs of doors failing to open and shut properly and a crack appearing in the kitchen door gave way to the sight of Jack's tractor disappearing as a hole opened up in the earth beneath it.

The Sugdens had to abandon the farmhouse that had been in the family for 140 years. Jack and Sarah found temporary accommodation in a chalet at the Holiday Village and at The Woolpack before moving, in April, to Hawthorn Cottage – which Joe had owned almost 20 years earlier and was now being sold by Bob Thornby in a dilapidated condition.

Jack and Joe kept the news from Annie, who was still in Spain, but she returned unexpectedly, felt deceived and refused to move to Hawthorn Cottage. Instead, she found temporary accommodation with Chris and Kathy Tate at The Mill. She added that she had turned down Leonard's proposal of marriage but might reconsider.

Peace was brought about when Amos suggested that Hawthorn Cottage be renamed Emmerdale.

Jack, son Robert and girlfriend Sarah Connolly make a fresh start in Hawthorn Cottage when subsidence forces them to leave the original farmhouse in 1993.

Annie capitulated and moved in, but then announced that she would marry Leonard and bought Tenant House, a cottage in the village. Meanwhile, Jack and Joe showed their skill by fitting a new kitchen at Hawthorn Cottage while Sarah went shopping to Harrogate with Annie.

Annie's Short-lived Marriage

Leonard and Annie's wedding went ahead at St Mary's Church on 28 October 1993, with the Revd Donald Hinton returning as a guest but taking the service after the Revd Johnson lost his voice. However, Annie and Leonard's time together was cut tragically short by the plane crash that devastated the village two months later.

As Joe drove the couple off to Leeds Bradford Airport for another winter break in Spain, he saw a wing piece from the plane falling from the sky, swerved and careered off the road. Leonard died immediately and Annie lay in a coma for three months. She regained consciousness only after Jack and Sarah took to the hospital their new baby daughter, Victoria, born on 31 March 1994. As a result, Annie was able to attend the couple's wedding the following month.

Another victim of the air disaster was Mark, who was sent to Whiteley's Farm by Joe to return a vacuum cleaner borrowed from Lynn Whiteley. Mark could be identified only by a watch that Annie had given him.

On the night of the disaster, Jack helped the emergency services through by erecting a make-shift bridge over the river with drainage pipes, using his tractor to lift them into place.

Joe Leaves For Ever

Joe failed to come to terms with the loss of stepson Mark and his own stepfather. When young Donna Windsor was injured while being given a ride on an Emmerdale tractor by Michael Feldmann and her mother threatened to sue the farm, Joe made a half-hearted suicide attempt with a shotgun.

During 1994, he finally chose to leave the village – renamed Emmerdale in the wake of the disaster in recognition of the Sugden family's contribution to the community – and join his mother in Spain. It was a shock when news came, on 6 June 1995, of Joe's death in a car crash. Annie brought his body home for burial in the village he had known for most of his life.

Because he did not leave a will, Joe's share of the farm automatically went to his mother, although she passed it on to his stepdaughter Rachel's newborn son, Joseph, to inherit on his eighteenth birthday. Shortly after the funeral, Annie proposed to Amos. They returned to Spain and married on 5 November.

Sarah Cheats on Jack

Jack and Sarah had the added trauma in 1994 of discovering, after Victoria's arrival home, that their newborn daughter had a hole in the heart. She was rushed back to hospital and, fortunately, survived. But, while staying there with Victoria, Sarah had an affair with a member of the hospital staff.

Although she did not want to lose Jack, Sarah then left Emmerdale with baby Victoria, hoping to trigger a response from him. Jack reacted by meeting her on neutral ground in York and the couple were reunited.

However, Jack suspected Sarah of having another affair when, the following year, she started working for university professor Andrew McKinnon, who was writing a book. Following her one day, Jack left son Robert alone in his car and returned to find him missing.

Jack and Sarah believed him to have been kidnapped and received telephone calls demanding £5000 for Robert's safe return. But the police traced the calls to Sam Dingle, who simply saw the Sugdens' misfortune as a means of making money.

In the event, Robert had gone off willingly with hermit Derek Simpson, a former paratrooper, and was under no threat. As the police search intensified, Simpson persuaded Robert to return to his parents.

Refuge for Rachel

Rachel and Joseph moved in briefly with Jack and Sarah in 1996 after Rachel walked out on husband Chris Tate. However, they returned to Chris and The Mill when Rachel gave her marriage another go, although the reconciliation only postponed the final day when they were to part.

On the Move Again

Less than four years after taking up residence in the new farmhouse, Jack and Sarah were on the move once more as bulldozers roared in to reduce the former Hawthorn Cottage to rubble to make way for the access road to Demdyke Quarry.

After moving out of the house in January 1997, the couple bought Woodside Farm and earmarked it for conversion. After a short time in a caravan next to the dilapidated farmhouse, Jack and Sarah moved temporarily into Annie's cottage, Tenant House, with Robert and Andy Hopwood, whom they had started fostering the previous December. They soon experienced difficulties with Andy, who had nowhere to live after his father was jailed and his grandmother died.

While at Tenant House, Jack decided that the work needed on Woodside Farm was too expensive, so he offloaded the property onto Tony Cairns, who had arrived with his family and was looking for a home in the village where his wife, Becky, had grown up.

Sarah felt guilty about selling Woodside Farm to the family, but Jack claimed that it was really a conversion job for middle-class incomers and persuaded Tony to buy it for £50,000 more than he had paid. Relying on Jack's honesty and commissioning only

Farm labourer Ned Glover is shocked to discover Jack having an affair with Rachel Hughes, his late brother Joe's stepdaughter.

a cheap survey, Tony was furious to discover later that the work needed, such as underpinning, would cost £50,000.

By then, Jack and Sarah had moved their brood to Melby's Farm, paying £170,000 at auction for a working farm that they could inhabit straight away. As before, they renamed it Emmerdale.

When Billy Hopwood was released from prison and found a farm labouring job, Andy went to live with him in a caravan. But Billy soon returned to a life of crime and Andy was left to his own devices. As a result, he moved in with Jack and Sarah on a more permanent basis.

Unfaithful Jack

A rift had developed between Jack and Sarah when Andy returned to his father. She had doubts about whether letting the boy go was wise, but he felt that they should give Billy a chance. Jack found solace in an affair with Rachel Hughes – his late brother Joe's stepdaughter – after she started working on the farm in 1997.

When Sarah eventually discovered Jack's infidelity, she threw him out. However, he did not pursue Rachel, and Sarah allowed him back when she wanted to provide a home for Andy again. It took a long time for the wounds to heal.

Another youngster joined the clan when Jack and Sarah took in 14-year-old Emma Cairns for a few months in 1998 after her parents moved to Germany. However, following a summer job at the Holiday Village, she left to join them.

Kathy's Diner

Downstairs (Business)		**Upstairs (Flat)**	
1995–8	Tearooms run by Kathy Tate (later Glover)	1995–7	Kathy Tate (later Glover), Dave Glover (1995, 1996), Nick Bates (1995–6), Alice Bates (1995, 1996–7)
1996–8	Wine bar run by Eric Pollard, plus Dee Pollard (1997–8)		
1998–	Diner run by Kathy Glover	1997–	Eric Pollard, Dee Pollard (1997–8)

CREATING REALITY

One building on the Harewood set that is almost identical to that previously used for filming in Esholt is the former tearooms and wine bar. Engraved in the lintel above the door is 'School House AD 1826', a legacy of the building's previous use in the story as the village primary school.

Eric and Dee Pollard, who ran the wine bar, moved into the upstairs flat after swapping Victoria Cottage with Kathy Glover, who ran the tearooms by day. When Pollard lost his licence to sell alcohol in 1998, Kathy bought him out and turned the business into an American-style diner.

'The only difference in the building compared with the previous one in Esholt is that we've put in a small playground area outside in place of a wall,' says designer Mike Long. 'The original idea was that, in the summer, Kathy could put tables out there and customers could enjoy tea on the terrace, overlooking the ford, the footbridge over the stream and the cricket pavilion.'

The studio set was one of the first that Mike designed, back in 1995. 'I've never been happy with the kitchen,' he says, 'because it was supposed to be altered in the story but that idea was dropped.

'Kathy decorated the tearoom area pretty-pretty after taking over the premises. When the wine bar started, we put the brightly coloured lights on the counter, which were always switched on when it was open. Since switching to a diner in August 1998, there's been a major change in the look. The colours are a light and a vivid blue, and we have replaced the tabletops with beechwood and put in Lloyd Loom furniture – the sort used in Victorian bedrooms.'

A separate set in a different part of the studio is used for the upstairs flat. 'Kathy's a pretty, well-presented lady, so the colour scheme was intended to reflect that,' says Mike of the yellow living room and lilac bedroom. 'When Pollard and Dee moved in, they didn't redecorate, but we put an oriental feel in because she was from the Philippines. That has gradually come out since she left him.'

Left *Kathy Tate's divorce settlement enables her to open the Old School Tea Rooms in 1995.*

Right *Dodgy Eric Pollard makes use of the tearoom premises in the evenings when he opens his wine bar.*

Built in 1846 by the benevolent Verney family, who owned the Miffield Estate, Beckindale's village school finally closed in the 1970s through lack of pupils. This meant that children had to travel to neighbouring Connelton. The building remained unused until 1995, when Kathy Tate became locked in a battle with Frank Tate over its purchase, after his son Chris had given her a £120,000 divorce settlement.

Kathy won the fight, moved into the upstairs accommodation in June and planned to turn the premises downstairs into tearooms. But she faced problems on discovering that an underground spring had flooded the basement, causing structural problems. These were solved when a builder dug deep and installed a pump. Eventually, the tearooms opened in August 1995, with Betty Eagleton and Dolores Sharp employed as waitresses, and it provided a new meeting place for villagers.

Love Triangle

Although Kathy had lost husband Chris to Rachel Hughes, she formed an unlikely friendship with Rachel, helped partly by her presence at The Mill when Rachel went into premature labour with son Joseph in June 1995. Kathy even became godmother to the baby, which shocked Chris.

Kathy herself was being romanced by Dave Glover, Frank Tate's young assistant farm manager who had been seduced by his employer's wife, Kim. Dave proposed to Kathy and he moved in with her in the flat above the tearooms, but she subsequently overheard Kim and Dave talking about their affair and agreed to marry him only if he left his job at Home Farm. In the event, once he made it clear that he was willing to do so, Kathy did not insist that Dave go through with it.

Kim twisted the knife by getting Kathy's brother,

Nick Bates, sacked from his job as gardener at Home Farm and thrown out of accommodation in the nursery flat, which he shared with his daughter Alice. As a result, Nick and Alice found accommodation with Kathy and Dave.

Nick was eventually reinstated at Home Farm, but Kathy was devasted to hear that Dave was seeing Kim again, called off their engagement and sent him packing.

Upstairs, Downstairs

When new chef Sean Rossi started work at the tearooms in early 1996, Betty did all she could to engineer romance between him and Kathy. Sean offered Kathy a shoulder to cry on when brother Nick was remanded in custody, awaiting trial after he shot and killed poacher Jed Connell at Frank Tate's fish farm in 1996.

Kathy's relationship with Sean had to take second place to her family troubles and business activities, but the chef warned off the dead poacher's accomplices when they started threatening her.

Downstairs changes during 1996 were dominated by Kathy accepting a business partnership with wheeler-dealer Eric Pollard, who in July opened a wine bar on the premises in the evenings. It was Pollard who, after stealing money from the tearooms, implied that Sean might have been responsible by revealing to Kathy that he had a criminal past.

When she confronted Sean, he turned aggressive and walked out. But Kathy later discovered that Sean had been jailed after being involved in a tragic accident in which his daughter had died.

Loved and lost

Kathy never lost her love for Dave, who believed himself to be the father of Kim's baby son, James, born in September 1996. When Frank would not let him near his wife, Dave returned to Kathy and, on hearing him telling Kim to stay out of his life, Kathy proposed. The couple married at Hotten Register Office in November and they started their life together in Kathy's flat.

But that life proved short – just four weeks – with Dave returning to Kim when the lady of the manor felt that she could build a new life with him and baby James away from Emmerdale. She tried to persuade Dave to do so, but he was torn between his two lovers.

Finally making up his mind at sister Linda's wedding reception on Christmas Eve, he left for Home Farm, where Kim had her bags packed, ready to go. During a confrontation with Frank outside, a fire started in the nursery, where James lay in his cot. Dave dashed back inside, rescued the baby and handed him out, only to be cut off by the flames as he himself attempted to escape.

Dave was rushed to hospital with severe injuries and died on Boxing Day from burns and lung damage. The love triangle was over, with no winners.

Brooding Barman

Another love triangle was that caused when Woolpack bar manager Terry Woods fell for postmistress Viv Windsor, who walked out on husband Vic when he discovered her infidelity. However, the affair ended, and when Terry was sacked by landlord Alan Turner he was taken on by Pollard as barman at the wine bar and lodged with Betty Eagleton and Seth Armstrong.

Working for Pollard made Terry realise what a reasonable boss he had previously enjoyed in Alan. Fed up with being treated as a dogsbody and having burned his bridges at the pub, Terry then planned to take a bar job in Leeds. But Alan persuaded him to return to The Woolpack as bar manager and he was glad to accept.

Guardian Angel

It was a shock when Nick was jailed for 10 years in 1997 for the shooting incident at the fish farm the previous year and three-times-wed Kathy found herself as a permanent guardian to Alice. But this

Kathy's marriage to cheating Dave Glover is short-lived, as he dies after saving lover Kim Tate's baby son James from a burning Home Farm.

ended the anxiety caused to Kathy shortly before the trial when Nick's new American girlfriend, Karen Johnson, had tried to befriend Alice and told the girl that she would be going to Boston with them after her father's release.

It appeared to be mutually convenient when Eric Pollard suggested swapping accommodation with Kathy after his marriage to Filipino Dee de la Cruz. So Kathy moved across the road to Victoria Cottage with Alice, Eric and Dee moved into the flat above the tearooms and wine bar.

Kathy Goes It Alone

Yet another love triangle appeared to come along when teenager Will Cairns was employed by Pollard as a waiter and developed a crush on Dee, who was flattered by his attention but insisted that she was married and would not cheat on her husband.

However, the marriage ended in April 1998 when Dee walked out on Pollard and returned to the Philippines after finding out that he had not been giving her letters and messages from her ailing mother, who then died.

Pollard's personal problems were added to when police raided the wine bar and he lost his licence for serving under-age drinkers. As a result, Kathy bought out his share in the business – while he continued living in the flat above – and she turned the premises downstairs into an American-style diner.

Tenant House

1993–6	Annie Sugden (later Kempinski and Brearly)	1997	Tony and Becky Cairns, Charlie Cairns, Will Cairns,
1996	Dave Glover, Kim Tate, Sean Rossi		Emma Cairns, Geri Cairns
1997	Jack and Sarah Sugden, Robert Sugden, Victoria Sugden, Andy Hopwood	1998–	Biff Fowler, Marlon Dingle, Jed Outhwaite (1998), Will Cairns

CREATING REALITY

The village house known as 'Annie's Cottage' after Annie Sugden bought it in 1993 became Tenant House when the new *Emmerdale* outdoor set was built at Harewood.

'The door and run of four windows in the front match the property we used in Esholt,' says designer Mike Long. 'Artstone was used for all the surrounds.' A date stone, inscribed '1671 TR', sits in the lintel above the door.

The studio set is simply furnished. 'It was dressed up a bit better when Annie used to live in the cottage,' says Mike. 'But, now that Annie's living away, it has just the basic furniture and is rented out – nothing special. Annie's son, Jack, doesn't do much to it.'

Tenant House stands next to Jacob's Fold, named after Annie's first husband, whose funeral opened the serial in 1972.

Annie Sugden marries second husband Leonard Kempinski in 1993 but loses him when he becomes a victim of the air disaster.

Annie Sugden bought herself a cottage in Beckindale in 1993 after announcing to her sons, Jack and Joe, that she planned to marry wealthy tax exile Leonard Kempinski, whom she had met while holidaying at Amos Brearly's retirement villa in Spain. This came shortly after Jack and his wife-to-be, Sarah Connolly, had to leave the original Emmerdale farmhouse because of subsidence and moved into Hawthorn Cottage. Annie eventually agreed to join them there, before surprising the family by buying her own house.

Leonard and Annie set 28 October as their wedding date and all appeared to be going smoothly until the Revd Johnson lost his voice and Donald Hinton – the village's last vicar, now returning as a guest 14 years after leaving – stepped in to take the ceremony at St Mary's Church.

Annie appeared to have found love again in her twilight years, but a happy future was cruelly taken away from her by the plane crash visited upon Beckindale in December 1993. Son Joe was driving the couple off to Leeds Bradford Airport so that they could fly to Spain for a mid-winter break, but part of the wing descending from the sky caused him to swerve off the road and crash, leaving Leonard dead and Annie unconscious.

Her other son, Jack, maintained a hospital vigil as Annie lay in a coma, on a life-support machine, for more than three months. His grave concern was alleviated when she regained consciousness as he and Sarah brought their new-born daughter, Victoria, to the hospital. Annie was able to attend the couple's subsequent wedding, in May 1994.

Leaving Beckindale for good, Annie settled in Spain and Joe followed her there, unable to come to terms with the loss of his stepson, Mark Hughes, in the air disaster. Annie returned to the newly named village of Emmerdale in 1995 to bring Joe's body back for his funeral, following his tragic death in a car crash.

After the funeral, Annie proposed to Amos Brearly. They returned to his villa in Spain and married there on 5 November. She returned to the village that she had known all her life only once more when, in 1996, she demanded that Jack sell the farm so that she could raise desperately needed money from her share.

Affair Under Annie's Roof

In Annie's absence, Jack and Sarah kept an eye on her cottage. Dave Glover moved in during April 1996 at the height of his affair with Kim, wife of lord of the manor Frank Tate.

Kim, who was pregnant, had persuaded him that the baby was his – although a blood test later proved otherwise – and he joined her at Home Farm. But, when he found the bickering between his lover and her husband too much to take, Dave grasped the opportunity to live elsewhere, having been disowned by his parents, Ned and Jan.

On his first evening at the cottage, Kathy came knocking at the door and was caught kissing him when Kim arrived, clutching a bottle of champagne. Kim appeared to win the battle for Dave and moved in with him, although he soon found himself out of his depth as he mixed in her social circle.

Kim's true self was revealed when Frank offered her £1 million to move back to Home Farm, put his name on the baby's birth certificate and live with him for the first year of the baby's life. Without revealing Frank's bribe, Kim told Dave she was returning to Frank because the baby was his. During July 1996, Dave took in tearooms chef Sean Rossi as a lodger.

Eventually, Dave returned to Kathy, the flames of love were rekindled and they married in November 1996, when Dave joined Kathy at the flat above her tearooms. The union finished little more than a month later, when Dave died after rescuing Kim's son, James, in a fire at Home Farm as he prepared to elope with her.

Halfway House

Annie's son, Jack, moved into Tenant House with wife Sarah and children Robert and Victoria in 1997 while they were waiting for conversion work to be completed at Woodside Farm, which was to replace the second Emmerdale farmhouse, knocked down to make way for an access road to Demdyke Quarry.

Also with the family was Andy Hopwood, the schoolboy they were fostering. But they had to cope with his anti-social behaviour, such as when he hit Donna Windsor after she taunted him about not having parents who wanted him and the time he broke Robert's Playstation birthday present. After attacking Donna again, at school, then landing a blow that left teacher Miss Cullen with a bloody nose, Andy was excluded from school for three weeks, with work to do at home.

Progress at Woodside Farm was similarly difficult. Eventually, Jack abandoned the costly job and sold the property to the incoming Cairns family while buying Melby's Farm at auction and moving in straight away.

When Tony Cairns discovered the extent of work needed at Woodside Farm he was furious, but he eventually accepted Jack and Sarah's offer to rent Tenant House. During the family's stay, 13-year-old daughter Emma decided to give up for adoption the baby she had given birth to in March 1997 and elder sister Charlie left the village after discovering that her ex-boyfriend, Greg Cox, was the baby's father. The family finally moved to Woodside Farm in November.

Dave Glover finds refuge at Tenant House, but lover Kim Tate follows him.

Bachelor Pad

In January 1998, Biff Fowler and Marlon Dingle – who had both become outcasts from their own families – squatted in the cottage. When Sarah Sugden discovered this, she threw them out. However, Kathy Glover – who had previously provided Biff with a shoulder to cry on during his marriage to Linda, which ended with her death in a car crash – persuaded Sarah to rent the house to the couple for £300 a month.

For a short time, they took in as lodger Jed Outhwaite when he was evicted from his ailing farm and needed somewhere to live. Later, teenager Will Cairns joined the pair after his parents moved to Germany.

Victoria Cottage

1984–90	Caroline Bates, Kathy Bates (1985–8), Nick Bates (1985–9)	1992–3	Elizabeth and Eric Pollard
1989–91	Alan Turner	1994–7	Eric Pollard, Dee Pollard (1997)
1991–2	Elizabeth Feldmann and Michael Feldmann	1997–	Kathy Glover, Alice Bates

CREATING REALITY

Like Seth and Betty's home next door, Kathy Glover's house – previously known as 17 Main Street – was given a name, Victoria Cottage, when the outdoor set was built on the Harewood estate.

'The windows are the same as they were in Esholt,' says designer Mike Long, 'but Kathy has four out of six panels glazed in the door. She also has a back garden, so Betty can see Kathy hanging out her knickers on the line!' The garden includes a modern, rotary washing line, in contrast to the traditional line that Betty uses.

When Kathy replaced Eric and Dee Pollard in the cottage, Mike took the opportunity to give the studio set a new look.

'There was a storyline where a boyfriend re-decorated the living room in a pretty-pretty style, which you would expect for Kathy,' he says. 'I also added a serving hatch from the kitchen because it was previously a small, rectangular living room, which was a bit boring. That also means we can shoot through the serving hatch to give us another angle.'

Caroline Bates, separated from schoolteacher husband Malcolm, arrived in Beckindale in 1984 to become secretary to Alan Turner, the boozing, gambling, womanising NY Estates manager who had pledged to turn over a new leaf after being threatened with dismissal by the Humberside-based property conglomerate's managing director, Christopher Meadows.

She moved into 17 Main Street, a tied cottage that went with the job, along with teenage children Kathy and Nick. In 1985, Caroline finally divorced estranged husband Malcolm after discovering that he was having an affair. Two years later, he and girlfriend Sonia had a baby son, William.

Work and Play

Kathy gave up her A-levels when Alan offered her a job with NY Estates as a farm worker in charge of the poultry unit at Home Farm. But she was distressed at seeing thousands of battery hens being reared there and walked out, finding part-time employment as a labourer at Emmerdale Farm, where she also helped Dolly Skilbeck to set up a farm shop. In addition, Kathy looked after Alan Turner and Joe Sugden's horses.

Kathy fell for Jackie Merrick, but their relationship was stormy and, in 1987, smooth-talking NY Estates trainee manager Tony Marchant – a wealthy relative of Christopher Meadows – tried to win her affections. Jackie responded by vandalising Tony's van, with the effect that Kathy realised his true feelings for her.

The couple became engaged and were married at St Mary's Church on 3 February 1988, with father Malcolm giving Kathy away, although a burst water pipe in the Bates household the night before the wedding destroyed her dress. Disaster was averted when Annie Sugden offered Kathy her own Edwardian wedding dress – which her mother had also worn – for the ceremony. Kathy and Jackie honeymooned in Tunisia and started married life in the attic at Emmerdale Farm before moving to 3 Demdyke Row.

Although the passion is intense and their relationship fiery, Kathy Bates eventually marries Jackie Merrick.

Nick the Drifter

After failing his A-levels, Kathy's younger brother, Nick, returned to school to retake them but soon lost interest and left. He landed a job as a porter at Hotten Market, working for auctioneer Sandie Merrick, but left after she was replaced by slimy Eric Pollard.

Nick then found employment as a gardener at Home Farm and fell for Leeds girl Clare Sutcliffe. When he witnessed a robbery at the village post office in 1988, Nick was hailed a hero after frightening off the robbers but gave in to temptation by taking some of the cash they dropped. He entrusted it to Clare, who was never seen again.

When Eric Pollard discovered Nick's hypocrisy, he blackmailed him into giving market details such as house sales and forced him to take part with Phil Pearce in the theft of antique fireplaces from Home Farm. Phil was jailed but Pollard, in his usual fashion, squirmed out of getting his just deserts through lack of evidence. Nick confessed everything to the police.

Business and Pleasure

Alan continued as manager of the Home Farm estate after NY Estates' departure in 1987. Caroline encouraged him to start a fish and game farm there two years later, shortly before Frank Tate bought Home Farm. Caroline became his partner in the new business, with its office based in her cottage, supplying fish to local restaurants and birds for its own shoots and others in the region.

Amorous Alan also finally made a conquest of Caroline after sleeping with her in the spring of 1989 and the couple planned a December wedding, with Henry Wilks earmarked as best man. However, the marriage plans were abandoned when Caroline had to leave for Scarborough in October to look after her sick mother.

She returned the following year to clear her belongings from the house, before leaving again for Scarborough. In 1991, after Alan had taken over the Woolpack pub, Caroline was back to demand compensation for her cottage, in which she had been a sitting tenant. Alan had been able to buy it

When Caroline Bates is appointed as Alan Turner's secretary, she makes a new home in her tied cottage and becomes very close to Alan.

as the fish and game farm's office only because they intended to live there together. In an attempt to evade the issue, Alan took Caroline on a picnic and once more asked her to marry him, but she insisted that she wanted a financial settlement, not a marriage proposal. Caroline has since made occasional return visits to the village.

New Appointments

Alan had made use of the government's Youth Training Scheme in 1990 to appoint young Elsa Feldmann as his secretary at the fish farm, her first job after leaving school. She was a conscientious worker, adept at keeping his books, and continued labouring at Keller Bottom Farm, Blackthorn, three miles out of Beckindale, which her widowed mother, Elizabeth Feldmann, rented until her inability to pay the rent on the ailing farm caused landlord Frank Tate to issue an eviction order in November 1990.

In the meantime, Elsa found herself expecting Nick Bates's baby and in January 1991, as she entered the later stages of her pregnancy, she handed over the secretarial job to her mother. In the same month, Alan became landlord of The Woolpack and made Elizabeth manager of the fish farm. She moved into 17 Main Street with son Michael in February.

On the family front, Elizabeth had to cope with Elsa giving birth prematurely to daughter Alice on the way to her planned Valentine's Day wedding – then walking out on Nick and later returning the baby to him – and son Michael's doomed engagement to Rachel Hughes.

After Elizabeth Feldmann takes over from Caroline as Alan Turner's manager of the fish farm, she falls for slimy Eric Pollard and marries him in 1992.

More Failed Advances

Following his rejection by Caroline Bates, Alan set his sights on Elizabeth and was frustrated to see her fall for Eric Pollard's smooth talk. Although Frank Tate took over the fish farm in 1992, Alan continued to run the game farm, with Elizabeth 'managing' it for him. He tried to warn Elizabeth off Pollard, but without success.

Elizabeth, however, began to have doubts about Pollard's claim to have changed his ways when correspondence addressed to 'Beckindale Antiques' began to arrive at her cottage and Pollard moved pieces of 'reserved' furniture there from the Hotten Market auction rooms for private sale.

Michael Goes off the Rails

Elizabeth's son, Michael, went through a difficult period. After the failure of the family farm, he was unemployed for a while until getting work at Emmerdale Farm. When Rachel Hughes was sacked from her receptionist's job at Tate Haulage,

Michael's commiserations led to romance, although he had a one-night stand with Zoë Tate during the early weeks of their relationship.

When Michael proposed marriage, Rachel accepted but subsequently began to wonder whether she was tying herself down too early in her life. When Rachel left to study at Leeds University, she and Michael began to drift apart. He took it very badly when she broke off the engagement.

Michael also suffered a setback in 1992 when he set his heart on becoming tenant at Winslow's Farm following the death of George Winslow, but landlord Frank Tate did not consider him to be experienced enough and decided to turn it into a heritage farm for the benefit of residents in the Holiday Village.

Going off the rails, Michael – who moved into the cottage extension at Emmerdale Farm with Mark Hughes – joined the Rt Hon. Neil Kincaid's stablehand, Steve Marshal, and his gang in a robbery at Home Farm, taking valuables and clubbing Joe Sugden unconscious when he disturbed them.

When Eric Pollard posed as a dodgy dealer meeting the gang as they tried to off-load the goods, he tipped off the police, who arrested them, although Michael was not there. However, when his mother married Pollard on 6 October 1992, Michael was taken away by police as the couple left church. He was later sentenced to four months in Roxleigh Prison for his part in the robbery.

Short-lived Marriage

Elizabeth and Eric were to have little more than a year together at the cottage. At first, it appeared as if she was exercising a calming influence on her husband, but she eventually came to see that he had not turned over the new leaf he had claimed to.

When Pollard conned young Mark Hughes into buying his ageing Triumph Spitfire for £900, Elizabeth forced him to return £300 to naïve Mark because the vehicle was little more than a rust-bucket. She also persuaded Pollard to hand over the rest of the profit after he had given Seth Armstrong just £20 for a tin full of valuable pre-decimal bank notes that he sold for £500. Then

Steve Marshal leaves prison and exacts revenge on Pollard, shopping him for a burglary at Home Farm, but Nick Bates rescues him from the flames of his car.

Elizabeth discovered that her husband had an £8000 overdraft and she insisted on taking control of the financial reins.

However, Elizabeth herself showed an unexpected side to her character when she discovered a muddy Roman bracelet at the fish farm, on Frank Tate's land, and let her husband sell it for £15,000, allowing her to pay off debts and set up a trust fund for granddaughter Alice.

On his release from jail in 1993, Steve Marshal exacted revenge on Pollard for fingering him for the Home Farm burglary. He tampered with the brakes on Pollard's car, causing the vehicle to crash on a bend, leave the road and go up in flames. Pollard performed another miraculous escape act when Nick Bates was on hand to rescue him from the inferno.

Bank on Eric?

During the same year, Elizabeth spotted anomalies in bank statements for the fish farm and paid the price by being sacked by Frank Tate after he discovered that the business chequebook – for which she was responsible – was being used for unauthorised payments. When Pollard managed to implicate Steve Marshal, who was no longer around to defend himself, Elizabeth was reinstated.

On a visit to the bank with her husband, Elizabeth heard him addressed as 'Mr Carter', the name in which the missing cheques had been made out. As Elizabeth became suspicious, Pollard tried to put the blame on her son, phoning PC Mitchum at Hotten police station with the tip-off that Michael owned the typewriter on which the bogus cheques had been typed.

When Elizabeth discovered what Pollard was up to and confronted him, he hurled the typewriter into the river to get rid of the 'evidence'. Then, on Christmas Eve, she finally threw Pollard out of the house. That evening, he visited Elizabeth at Nick Bates's cottage in Demdyke Row, where she was babysitting Alice. After a row, she stormed out and was killed by the devastation wrought on Beckindale by the horrific plane crash. Eric was seen later that night walking dementedly around the wreckage in a vain attempt to find her body. Elizabeth had disappeared, along with the truth about the cheque fraud.

More Skeletons

In the wake of his mother's death, Michael was convinced that his stepfather had used the plane crash as a cover for murdering her, suspicions confirmed in him by Pollard's insistence that Elizabeth's body be cremated and not buried. In the event, she was buried along with the other victims of the disaster.

Another incident revealed one of Pollard's best-kept secrets. His first wife, Eileen – using the surname Pollock – successfully blackmailed him for some of the insurance money on Elizabeth's life, threatening to tell the police that he had married bigamously. A divorce was also set in motion.

In his own money-making fashion, Pollard sanctimoniously presented the disaster fund with £1500 from the sale of an oil painting donated to it – after selling it for £175,000 – but Frank Tate uncovered this fraud on reading about the sale in *The Times*.

Michael continued in his belief that Pollard was responsible for his mother's death and, during a heated exchange in the cottage, planted a punch on Pollard's jaw that left him lying unconscious on the sofa. Worried that he had killed his stepfather, Michael took Pollard's keys and drove off in his car, which was later found at the airport. Michael was never seen again and Pollard – who recovered after a short spell in hospital – was relieved that this thorn in his side was no longer around.

Sharp Practices

Turning to another money-making venture, Pollard teamed up with Councillor Hawkins, from Hotten, with a view to setting up an open prison on widow Betty Eagleton's land. When Frank Tate led villagers in a campaign against the plan, Pollard persuaded her to let it out for a rave party, saying that she would make a profit, but he intended to ensure otherwise and force her to sell.

The event, in the summer of 1994, turned into a disaster, with Ben Dingle dying after provoking a fight with Luke McAllister. Betty was left with debts of £19,000, but she still refused to sell the land – until Frank Tate eventually took it off her hands.

Pollard swiftly moved on to another scheme, planning and executing a robbery of valuable artefacts at stately Briardale Hall, which netted him £150,000 worth of goods, while securing an alibi by arranging a dinner date with Alan Turner and spiking his drink with drugs so that he would fall asleep.

He also took advantage of Alan following the tragic death of the pub landlord's wife, Shirley, which led Alan to hit the bottle and start gambling. Offering his 'help' in financial matters, Pollard fiddled the books to make it appear that Shirley had been dishonest. In doing so, he almost persuaded Alan to accept a £20,000 loan, with The Woolpack as security. But he received his comeuppance when Frank Tate had Pollard's car crushed in front of the pub's customers and Caroline Bates ditched him in disgust after a short romance.

Into the Arms of the Law

Another short-lived affair came in the unlikely form of WPC Barbara Metcalfe in 1995, but that ended when her estranged husband, Harry, won her back after mounting a surveillance operation on Pollard's house that led village gossip Betty Eagleton to think that the police were finally going to give the elusive crook his come-uppance.

During his brief relationship with the policewoman, Pollard was more careful about his dodgy dealings. While organising an antiques auction in the village hall in partnership with Woolpack manager Terry Woods, Sam Dingle undertook a house clearance for Pollard but mistakenly entered 40 Skipdale Road instead of No 14 and took the contents to the hall. On discovering the mistake, Pollard ordered Sam to return everything.

An Unlikely Host

Pollard appeared to find an honest way of making a living when he persuaded Kathy Tate to enter a business partnership. She had opened her tearooms in Emmerdale in August 1995 and he saw the potential to make more money from the enterprise by starting a wine bar on the premises in the evenings, which he did the following July.

Then Pollard went on a mysterious holiday to the Philippines and returned to Emmerdale harbouring the secret that he had become engaged to 27-year-old Filipino waitress Dee de la Cruz. When she arrived in the village on Valentine's Day 1997, tongues started wagging.

But Pollard showed himself to be besotted with Dee and the couple married on 1 May that year, with Sam Dingle acting as their chauffeur after the ceremony at Hotten Register Office. Dee became invaluable in helping Pollard to run the wine bar. The couple soon moved into the flat above it when Kathy agreed to a swap and moved into Victoria Cottage, taking her back to the house where she had first lived in the village.

Changes Afoot

New love appeared to come into Kathy's life shortly afterwards when she met suave Doug Hamilton. She even continued the romance when he confessed to being married. But this proved to be a cover for the reality that he was gay and had a boyfriend called Richard. When Kathy found out, she refused to see Doug again.

During 1998 Kathy was able to concentrate on work, planning to convert the tearooms into a diner after Pollard lost his alcohol licence. She bought his share of the business while he continued to live in the flat above.

Pollard genuinely seems to love new wife Dee de la Cruz and eventually swaps accommodation with Kathy Tate.

Keepers Cottage

1995–   Betty Eagleton and Seth Armstrong   Lodgers: Ronnie Slater (1995), Biff Fowler (1995–6), Linda Glover (1995), Tom Bainbridge (1996–7), Terry Woods (1997), Paddy Kirk (1997–8)

CREATING REALITY

Pensioners Seth Armstrong and Betty Eagleton's terraced house at 19 Main Street, next to the post office, was renamed Keepers Cottage when the Harewood set was built, because Seth had for many years been a gamekeeper in Emmerdale.

'Most small Dales villages don't have road names or house numbers,' explains production designer Mike Long, who has kept the windows as in the previous Esholt location but treated the couple to a better front door – a six-panel one with two of the panels in glass.

A lobby and stairs have been built inside the door for filming Seth and Betty entering or leaving. Roses were planted to run up the outside wall to create the right kind of look for the cottages' inhabitants. 'We wanted it very flowery and different from Kathy Glover's house next door, all hollyhocks and bird-houses,' says Mike.

Inside, the windows have deep reveals to allow cameras to catch Betty snooping on events outside from over the net curtains.

The studio set comprises a living room awash with colour and props, plus a small kitchen. 'We spent a lot of time on props, such as all the china dogs, and gave Betty and Seth a nice, old-fashioned fabric for the sofa. It's actually a Sanderson fabric, which they probably couldn't afford, but it looked so good visually that we decided to go for it.'

Following the death of her husband, Wally, and her reacquaintance with old flame Seth Armstrong, Betty Eagleton moved into Keepers Cottage in February 1995, renting it from the Home Farm estate. But it took Betty a few days to persuade Seth to move in with her permanently as the plucky pensioners decided to live together without getting married. She was able to live with Seth's frequent disappearances to The Woolpack and proved herself capable of keeping him in check.

Wartime Sweethearts

Seth, who had become gamekeeper at Home Farm in 1978 after working as an odd-job man at the local school, had met Betty again after Wally's death in November 1993, just 10 months after the death of his own wife, Meg.

During the Second World War, Betty had been courted by both Seth and Wally. When she had to choose between the two, she opted for Wally. Meeting each other again gave both Betty and Seth the chance to look forward to life together in their old age.

Betty's house provided a refuge for Seth from the horrific plane crash that occurred over Beckindale at the end of that year. With his cottage in Demdyke Row destroyed, Seth lived in a hut on the game reserve, then at The Mill – home of Chris and

Kathy Tate – before being offered the job of heritage farm warden by Frank Tate and accommodation with Betty in a caravan on Emmerdale Farm land. Betty, meanwhile, found a job as housekeeper to Dr Bernard McAllister and his wife, Angharad.

When the Dingles vandalised the caravan, Seth and Betty temporarily moved into the farmhouse. They planned to marry in December 1994 but, on their wedding day, decided there was no point in exchanging vows at their time of life. Instead of the wedding breakfast, they staged a 1944-style fancy-dress knees-up to mark the fact that they would have married 50 years earlier if Betty had chosen Seth instead of Wally.

Seth Armstrong and Betty Eagleton opt for a Forties party instead of getting married, deciding they are too old to bother with such formalities.

After moving into Keepers Cottage, Betty landed a job as waitress at The Old School Tea Rooms, opened by Kathy Tate in the summer of 1995. Working in one of the village's meeting points is ideal for Betty, who also became cleaner at The Woolpack and is the community's most prolific gossip.

String of Lodgers

Seth and Betty have played host to a string of lodgers at Keepers Cottage, starting with Ronnie Slater, father of Woolpack manageress Britt Woods. Britt's husband, Terry, believed him to be dead and was shocked when his wife eventually revealed that Ronnie had abused her as a child. Ronnie left and Britt walked out on Terry for a new life in York.

Biff Fowler, Seth's young drinking partner, stayed for a year until moving out in July 1996 to live with his fiancée, Linda Glover, in a cottage on the Home Farm estate, where he worked. After agreeing to a

Lodger Tom Bainbridge's seduction of pupil Kelly Windsor scandalises village gossip Betty.

'no sex' relationship, Biff proposed the following month and the couple married at the end of the year. Linda had also stayed briefly at Keepers Cottage, in December 1995.

More contentiously, schoolteacher Tom Bainbridge took lodgings with Seth and Betty the following year and seduced 16-year-old schoolgirl Kelly Windsor. Although nothing ever took place under her roof, Betty was outraged to see Tom kissing Kelly at a New Year's Eve party. In January 1997, Tom was forced to move school and Kelly dropped him after catching him in bed with another pupil.

Terry Woods had also been a bit of a bad boy, having an affair with Kelly's mother, Viv, before losing his job as manager at The Woolpack and finding accommodation at Keepers Cottage in March 1997. However, his stay was short. After working at Eric Pollard's wine bar, where he was often reduced to being a dogsbody and did not re-

ceive overtime pay, he planned to take a bar job in Leeds. But Alan Turner persuaded him to return to the pub as manager, with the incentive of taking ten per cent of the profits.

Vet Paddy Kirk had two spells with Seth and Betty. He arrived in Emmerdale to help out Zoë Tate at her surgery in early 1997 as she spent much of her time dealing with family business matters after her father, Frank, was remanded in custody on a charge of killing wife Kim, who subsequently reappeared. Betty fussed over Paddy and made sandwiches for his lunch every day.

When Zoë put Steve Marchant in charge of business affairs at Home Farm and returned to working full-time in April, she could find him no work, so Paddy left for Cumbria. This was a blow to Woolpack barmaid Mandy Dingle, who had fallen for him. But the pair were reunited when he returned to work for Zoë later in the year. Paddy finally moved out of Keepers Cottage to live with Mandy in the outhouse conversion at Wishing Well Cottage in February 1998.

Post Office and Village Stores

1973	Amy Postlethwaite (tenant, living in)	1976	Norah Norris
1973–4	Alison Gibbons (living in) in partnership with Henry Wilks	1988	Mrs Robson
1974–6	Liz Ruskin (not living in but working for Henry Wilks)	1993–	Vic and Viv Windsor, with Kelly, Scott and Donna Windsor

CREATING REALITY

Vic and Viv Windsor's post office and village stores, with accommodation above, was re-created on the Harewood set with a freezer cabinet and shelving unit in view when the door is opened so that part of the interior can be seen when filming outside. They are replicated in the studio for scenes that take place inside the shop.

'We put postcards and a pile of walking sticks outside the door to give the feeling of a real shop in the region,' says designer Mike Long. 'The Yorkshire Dales National Park has allowed us to use a lot of its literature and graphics inside and in the front window. A lot of little post offices in the Dales are information points for the National Park.

'We've also had mock cheeses from the Wensleydale Creamery – polystyrene wrapped in wax – items from Swaledale Woollens and a postbox from the Post Office. And, yes, there is real booze in the bottles. It's actually quicker for companies to supply the real thing than to mock it up. '

The studio set was changed slightly after outdoor filming began at Harewood. 'Previously, the view in through the door had to match the post office we used in Esholt,' says Mike. 'The shelving unit that you see was blocking out anyone behind it, so I turned it through 90 degrees. The counter area has not changed at all, but we have to keep the props up to date because packaging does change quite frequently. '

Behind the counter, a door leads via a storeroom into the back room of the shop on this composite set. 'I like it when you get rooms leading into other rooms,' says Mike. 'It's much more real and helps actors and directors with the flow of movement and dialogue.'

Alison Gibbons takes over the shop, in partnership with Henry Wilks, when Amy Postlethwaite leaves Beckindale.

Amy Postlethwaite, who leased Beckindale's post office and village stores from lord of the manor George Verney, found help in running it when widow Alison Gibbons started working there in 1973 after a stint as barmaid at The Woolpack earlier in the year.

Although Alison harboured the secret that she had a criminal record – for shoplifting – she soon became popular in Beckindale and agreed to be godmother to Matt Skilbeck's twins, Sam and Sally, following the tragic death of his wife, Peggy, just three months after their birth.

Alison also became active in the church choir at about the same time as Henry Wilks joined it, having arrived in Beckindale from Bradford only the previous year himself after retiring as a wool merchant.

When, in 1973, Amy became too ill to carry on at the shop, she gave Alison the chance to take over the lease. Henry and Alison agreed to try to buy the freehold in partnership and, to the surprise of some villagers, George Verney agreed, but he regarded Henry as an upstart and insisted that Alison keep a controlling interest. This still left Henry with financial stakes in Emmerdale Farm, The Woolpack and the village shop.

Alison's Suitors

Alison found herself the subject of Amos Brearly, Henry Wilks and Matt Skilbeck's attentions. Amos's main motive was to satisfy brewery Ephraim Monk's preference for married publicans in its establishments. Henry tried to take his business partnership at the shop even further when he asked Alison to marry him, but she turned him down.

Matt seemed to get closer to Alison, initially using the excuse of his daily trips to the shop to deliver eggs from Emmerdale Farm. Mother Annie realised that Matt had more on his mind than business sales when he invited Alison to tea at the farm in 1974.

He then took her to spend some time with his children, who were looked after by his Aunt Beattie and Uncle Ben in Blackfell, three miles away. Matt's aunt and uncle felt that Alison would make an excellent mother for the twins, but the couple drifted apart, realising that their relationship was nothing more than a friendship at a time when they were both in need of support.

Traveller and Travels

Alison had previously also enjoyed the company of traveller Dryden Hogben, who was employed as a handyman at Emmerdale Farm after he started camping on land there. While Henry had plied her with wine and Matt was to enjoy afternoon tea with her, 'Dry' took Alison to a transport café 12 miles away, on the Leeds road, where the pair enjoyed a slap-up meal on a plastic tablecloth.

Alison was concerned that 'Dry', who clearly had a sharp mind, was wasting his life, but he eventually disappeared from under everyone's eyes in The Woolpack when a woman called Celia arrived there looking for him. It turned out that he had jilted her at the altar and a letter to Matt later revealed that 'Dry' had fled to Ireland.

When Alison herself moved to Jersey in September 1974 to start a new business, Henry bought her share of the shop, thereby owning it outright. Henry found a shop assistant in Liz Ruskin, wife of Beckindale's vicar. In 1976, when

Edward Ruskin retired and he and Liz left the village, Norah Norris took over the shop.

It's all change as the Windsor family from London – Vic and Viv, with children Scott, Kelly and Donna – move north to take over the village stores and post office in 1993.

Daylight Robbery

In June 1988, when Mrs Robson ran the shop, young Nick Bates was hailed a hero after foiling a raid on the post office, but he could not resist taking some of the cash that was dropped by the robbers. When he entrusted it to his girlfriend, Clare Sutcliffe, she disappeared to Leeds. Nick was then blackmailed by Eric Pollard and Phil Pearce, who found out what he had done, but he gained his revenge by shopping them for stealing antique fire-places from Home Farm.

Sharp Reawakening

In the summer of 1993, a family of Londoners bought the village stores and post office after moving north to get away from crime on an East End overspill estate and find a healthy environment for bringing up children.

Cockney Vic Windsor put his redundancy money from Ford's Dagenham plant together with the cash that wife Viv received from her late father's flat

and bought the shop, later getting a licence for off-sales. Each had a child from their first marriage – Vic's daughter, Kelly, 12, born to his teenage sweetheart, who married him but later died, and Viv's son, Scott, 13, by her ex-husband, Reg Dawson – and the couple had one child together, daughter Donna, eight.

Vic yearned to live somewhere as picturesque as childhood weekends he recalled in Epping Forest. A series of violent incidents on the estate where the Windsor family lived, including one in which a child was fatally stabbed, spurred him on to look for a safer, healthier environment. Vic believed he had found it in Beckindale.

But the Windsors made an inauspicious start on their first visit to the village, showing themselves up as townies not used to the ways of the country-side. Vic – fan of rock 'n' roll stars from the 1950s such as Elvis Presley and Bill Haley – speeded along the roads in his pride and joy, a lovingly preserved Ford Zephyr, causing Kim Tate's horse, Dark Star, to rear up and race off. He also made himself unpopular by leaving gates open so that cows got out.

Worst of all, Vic put his own life in danger while taking the children out for a walk on the moors. He lost his footing on a grassy bank and fell into a freezing river, with the fast-moving current dragging him into a clump of foliage that trapped his leg. The teenagers ran for help, but in completely the wrong direction.

Fortunately, Luke McAllister and Biff Fowler heard Vic's panic-stricken cries for help while they were out hill climbing. Biff waded into the icy water but was unable to free Vic. He then raced for help and found Jack and Joe Sugden, who rushed their bow saw to the scene, where Joe managed to cut Vic free from the foliage. To complete the rescue, Luke managed to find the Windsor children. The family were learning the lessons of country life fast.

Troublesome Times

Scott Windsor failed to adjust to rural Beckindale, however, and found problems fitting in at school, where he became involved in fights. He did enjoy joining Michael Feldmann, Seth Armstrong's newly appointed assistant gamekeeper, in his work. But, after an incident involving poachers left him with a gunshot wound in his left arm, Vic stopped Scott's only rural pleasure.

Aching for the life he had left behind in London, Scott ran away on Guy Fawkes' Night 1993, joined friends on the Thamesmead housing estate where he had previously lived and found accommodation there with his Aunt Gina.

Vic rushed to London and, after taking Scott on a nostalgic trip down Memory Lane, persuaded him to return to Beckindale and give life there a chance. But Scott soon found himself the target of school bully Glen, who stole goods from the shop and coerced Scott into joyriding in Vic's Ford Zephyr, which ended up with him crashing it and Glen forcing Scott to implicate Michael Feldmann.

Eventually, Michael forced Scott to own up and he confessed all to his father, who took him to do the same with Inspector Ramsey at Hotten police station. Vic's silver lining came when he bought a Lotus Cortina Mk II, which desperately needed rebuilding – and a vintage motorcycle from the late Wally Eagleton's yard.

There was more trouble when younger sister Donna was offered a ride on Michael Feldmann's tractor on Emmerdale Farm. The vehicle toppled over and left Donna trapped in the wreckage, injured. Mother Viv was insistent that the family should sue the Sugdens for damages.

This came shortly after the deaths of Joe Sugden's stepson, Mark Hughes, and his mother's new husband, Leonard Kempinski, as a result of the air disaster, and Joe could take no more. Vic found him in the stables with a shotgun and realised that Joe was contemplating taking his life. He persuaded him to change his mind and insisted that there would be no legal action. For once, common sense prevailed.

Viv's Worst Nightmare

Trouble brewed for the Windsors when Scott's father, Reg Dawson, was released from jail and arrived at the post office bearing gifts for Viv and quoting the Bible. He insisted that his former wife's marriage to Vic was not blessed by God and they were committing a mortal sin by living together.

Keen to see Scott reunited with his father, Viv allowed Reg access to their new home, until he made it clear that he wanted her back. Vic managed to persuade him to leave by saying that the police had pointed out to him that a parolee was not allowed on post office premises. On leaving, Reg promised that he would return.

When he did so, in June 1994, it was in the most shocking way. With two other masked accomplices, he staged a bungled raid on the post office, just as the villagers were coming to terms with the plane disaster of six months earlier. Before leaving the post office, Reg turned on all the gas taps, causing an explosion that wrecked the premises.

The armed men took Viv hostage and went on the run, also grabbing Shirley Turner – recently married to Woolpack landlord Alan – and using her Range Rover as their getaway vehicle. During the shoot-out at the pub, Alan was hit by a stray bullet, leaving him wounded in hospital.

The raiders, whose numbers were reduced to two when one gunman crashed the escape car, then took Viv and Shirley to Home Farm, which was soon surrounded by armed policemen. Reg then accidentally shot dead his other accomplice after mistaking him for a policeman.

As he moved to shoot Viv, Shirley intervened to protect her and ended up taking the full force of the bullet herself. When police marksmen stormed the house, Reg was killed. Shirley, and Reg's partner in crime also lay dead.

Viv insisted on attending Reg's funeral, against Vic's wishes, so that she could bid good riddance to the man who had twice ruined her life.

Torn Off a Strip

Vic thought it a good wheeze when he and Terry Woods, who had arrived at The Woolpack with wife Britt to manage the pub for Alan Turner, organised strippers to appear at the 1995 Emmerdale Sportsmen's Dinner in the village hall. When Viv and Britt found out, they decided to sabotage the evening by stepping in for the strippers, walking off stage and throwing buckets of water over their husbands.

Step Inside, Love

The following year, Vic's friendship with Terry was torn apart by the former rugby player's affair with Viv, which began after the pair started dancing lessons at the village hall. Although the relationship was initially platonic, Vic was incensed to see a reference in the *Hotten Courier* to them as the dancing couple 'Mr and Mrs Terry Woods' and daughter Kelly presumed that they must be having an affair.

But that only happened when Terry offered Viv a shoulder to cry on following a row with Vic about her son, Scott, after he was caught stealing a pension book from the post office. Vic was adamant that the boy should be despatched to

Viv cheats on Vic when dancing classes with Terry Woods lead to an affair.

London to live with his aunt, but Viv insisted that she would leave with him unless Vic backed down.

Eventually, in September 1996, Scott left home to join the Army at Catterick. This gave Viv the chance to accompany him on his journey there, before joining Terry at a nearby hotel. Vic did not find out about his wife's infidelity until two months later when he burst in on Viv and Terry together as he brought Scott back on a surprise visit.

Unrepentant, Viv packed her bags and moved in with Terry at The Woolpack. However, she agreed to help Vic out at the post office in the busy run-up to Christmas, although both made it clear that this was only a business arrangement. Eventually, Terry ended the affair after a fling with *Hotten Courier* reporter Helen Ackroyd, and Viv realised that she had been used. But it was a long time before Viv and Vic's marriage returned to normal. 'You latched on to me while your last old man went to jail,' he told

Kelly seduces Chris Tate in an attempt to get out of her pregnancy dilemma.

her. 'I saved you from being a sad old cow with a season ticket to Wormwood Scrubs.'

Teacher's Pet

Kelly reacted badly to her stepmother's affair and totally rejected her, throwing a sixteenth-birthday present back in her face. Then Kelly developed a crush on one of her teachers, Tom Bainbridge, who allowed it to develop into a relationship. Local gossip Betty Eagleton – also Tom's landlady – witnessed the pair kissing at a party as Emmerdale saw in the New Year.

On discovering this latest time-bomb, Vic blew a fuse and complained to Tom's headmaster, with the result that the amorous teacher was forced to move school. Kelly exacted revenge on her father by secretly going with Tom to Stockport, but she came back – alone – after returning early from a waitressing job one day to discover him in bed with a fifth-former from his new school.

From the Frying Pan...

Kelly found a job during the summer of 1997 as a chalet maid at the Holiday Village, where an enemy of hers from school, Lyn Hutchinson, already worked. 'I've got my reputation to think about,' Lyn screamed at Biff Fowler, who then had responsiblity for managing the Holiday Village. 'I'm not working with that cockney slapper!'

Chris Tate, their boss, eventually stopped the feuding and the pair began to get on better together. Then Kelly wheedled her way into becoming Chris's personal assistant, which earned derision from his stepmother, Kim.

Although she saw Home Farm labourer Roy Glover on a casual basis, Kelly dated whiz-kid computer buff Will Cairns and persuaded him to fix the business computer there to put an extra £200 in her pay packet – which she promptly blew on staging a party. Chris eventually found out and said he would overlook her misdemeanour – if she were nice to him.

Kelly began to play a dangerous game when, in November 1997, she had a one-night stand with Biff – Roy's brother-in-law, who was still grieving the death of his wife, Linda – became pregnant, seduced Chris, then told him that the baby was his.

She saw this as an escape route, expecting Chris to pay for an abortion. But, seeing this as his last chance to father a second child, he insisted that she keep the unborn baby and he would stand by her. Also, Kelly – young enough to be his daughter – made him feel wanted once more. As a result, Kelly moved into the nursery flat at Home Farm, to the shock of Kim and many others in the village.

But a skirmish with Kim as Kelly tried on one of her dresses for a party given by Chris to impress clients ended up with Kelly falling down the stairs outside Kim's bedroom and miscarrying. Chris was devastated and Kelly, having lost the baby, realised that she had really wanted it.

She returned to her family, with Vic ordering Chris to keep away, and took a job as receptionist at Zoë Tate's veterinary surgery. The Windsor family seemed complete after the return of son Scott in 1998.

In the Studio

The post office and village stores was first featured in 1973. After events of the following year, it was not seen again until a brief appearance in 1988, when Nick Bates foiled an attempted robbery.

It came to the fore again when the Windsor family arrived from London to take over in 1993. Since then, it has become one of the village's main meeting places.

The most dramatic storyline featuring the post office was the raid of 1994, which included an explosion after one of the masked gunmen turned on the gas taps. Special-effects designer Ian Rowley managed to stage the explosion at the real-life post office in the village of Esholt without causing any damage to the building.

It was created by removing the window and door frames, replacing them with air-tight boxes and injecting silo blasters with propane gas, which was then ignited. Flames and smoke poured out as the cameras rolled and, 20 minutes after the Esholt postmaster had closed shop, he was able to open for business again without any damage.

A bungled raid on the post office by Viv's former husband, Reg Dawson, results in an explosion after he turns on the gas taps.

Smithy Cottage

1972–4	Frank Blakey, plus Janie Blakey (1973–4)	1995–	Zoë Tate, plus Emma Nightingale (1995–6), Susie Wilde (1996), Sophie Wright (1997), Kelly Windsor (1998)

CREATING REALITY

Zoë Tate's house and adjoining veterinary surgery are at Smithy Cottage, which in the story started life as the village forge and in real life is very similar, inside and out, to the building previously used in Esholt.

Scenes in the surgery reception and operating theatre are filmed inside part of the real-life Harewood set, but a studio set is used for Zoë's living room and kitchen-dining room. When location filming was done in Esholt, the cottage interiors were shot there, too.

'The Harewood building is much bigger than the Esholt one was,' says designer Mike Long, 'mainly because the previous one was far too small and, as this location is used a lot, it had to be increased. Also, I've added an extension to the surgery to act as a recovery room.

'In Esholt, we had turned the cottage – which was previously used as a store, full of gardening equipment, spiders and mice – from what was basically a hovel with a solid concrete floor into a living room and a kitchen-dining room. We kept the rustic stone interior, but had to repair the roof, put a damp-proof course in, lay a smoother concrete floor and build a fireplace because there wasn't one.'

In the studio, the cottage living room and kitchen-dining room have been replicated, using the same furnishings and props, including a tapestry over the fireplace whose tassels frayed away in Esholt.

'I found it in a carpet shop in Horsforth when we were decorating the Esholt location,' says Mike. 'It's actually a door curtain, used as a fly screen – it had long tassels hanging over the door to keep the flies out. The couple in Esholt only used the cottage at weekends and, once, had a roaring fire and we lost all the tassels.'

The studio set's living room has a door leading into the surgery with a screen in front that is replicated on the Harewood set so that people can be seen entering and leaving. The post office and The Woolpack are painted on a backdrop positioned behind the living room window.

Left *Blacksmith Frank Blakey and wife Janie are the last residents to live in the village forge before its conversion more than 20 years later.*

Right *Lesbian vet Zoë Tate enjoys a joint housewarming-birthday party when she moves into Smithy Cottage with her partner, Emma Nightingale*

Frank Blakey, Beckindale's peace-loving blacksmith, both lived and worked in the forge that he rented from local squire George Verney. He was joined there by Janie Harker – sister of Jack Sugden's first wife, Pat – when the couple married in March 1973.

When Dale Properties, a company in which Verney had a majority shareholding, tried to evict Frank, Jack presumed that the local landowner was behind the move because Frank, opposed to blood sports, had refused to shoe the horses of his hunt. He tipped off the *Hotten Courier* newspaper, which ran a story under the headline 'Anti-Blood Sport Blacksmith Victimised by Landlord'. In fact, Verney had been unaware of the eviction attempt and meted out a public horsewhipping to Jack, who was also having an affair with Verney's wife, Laura. In 1974, Frank decided to change career, take up teaching and move away from Beckindale with Janie.

Labour of Love

Emmerdale's forge found new life in April 1995 when local vet Zoë Tate bought it for use as a home and surgery, with her lesbian lover – designer Emma Nightingale, who had arrived in the village to give The Woolpack a new look – masterminding the conversion, which became Smithy Cottage.

The interior of the forge was transformed into a comfortable home, with beautiful beams and a fireplace whose design was based on the original furnace, and the surgery was located in the adjacent building, which until the 1920s had been the village wash-house.

Zoë, who had previously set up her own veterinary practice at her father Frank's heritage farm after working for Martin Bennett's practice in Hotten and doing a brief stint as a flying vet in New Zealand, had only recently discovered her sexuality after dating Archie Brooks and realising that she could not sleep with him – or any other man. But many villagers were shocked. Teenagers Roy Glover and Scott Windsor even daubed graffiti on the door of Smithy Cottage – but gave themselves away with their spelling of 'lesbeans'.

Zoë Beats Off Attack

Four months after moving into the old forge, Zoë was called out on business by farmer Ken Adlington, on the outskirts of Emmerdale – and suffered the ordeal of an attempted rape after Adlington suggested that she needed a man to sort out her sexuality. Zoë fought him off but was astonished when police refused to press charges because his wife, Margaret, gave him an alibi. This led Zoë to mount a campaign against the farmer so that locals would know what had happened. At the same time, Zoë's father, Frank, and Ned Glover warned Adlington to stay out of the village.

Linda's Abortion Scare

Linda Glover, receptionist at the vet's surgery, also found herself in danger in 1995 on discovering that she was pregnant by Lady Weir's two-timing son, Danny. In a successful attempt to abort the unborn baby, Linda used a lethal injection of horse tranquillisers from the surgery – but ended up seriously ill in hospital.

Gay Wedding

Zoë and Emma caused a further storm in the village when, in 1996, Emma proposed that their relationship should be cemented with a formal blessing. Woolpack landlord Alan Turner was one of those who made clear their disapproval.

Although the couple exchanged vows and rings at a hotel ceremony on 16 May, Zoë ditched Emma before the reception was over in favour of Emma's former partner, hairdresser Susie Wilde, who turned up several weeks earlier and caused friction. Emma left Emmerdale, but Zoë's new romance was short-lived as a result of Susie's infidelity.

The Wright Girl?

Zoë found new love with Sophie Wright, who was hired in 1996 as live-in nanny to her half-brother, James, at Home Farm. Theirs appeared to be a stable relationship, which flourished after Sophie moved into Smithy Cottage with Zoë, having found life impossible with Chris Tate following his father's spell in prison on remand.

More arduously, Sophie endured the attentions of Butch Dingle, who was obsessed with her. He stalked Sophie and hoaxed Zoë into going on a callout so that he could confront her inside Smithy Cottage. Sophie feared for her life as Butch flew into a rage and smashed a photograph of Zoë. However, she defused the situation and Butch's father, Zak, ensured she would be left alone in future.

Although she had slept with Butch twice while drunk, Sophie had no interest in him. She and Zoë even talked about having their own baby and saw a counsellor with a view to doing so by artificial insemination. However, Sophie battled to come to terms with her sexuality and left both Zoë and the village after little more than a year.

Supporting Cast

Caught up in the shenanigans between her father, Frank, and stepmother, Kim, Zoë could always be relied on to support Frank in his business dealings through her share in the family business. Her father had shown surprising support when she originally revealed her sexuality to him and it was a great shock, on returning to Home Farm with Sophie in May 1997, to find him dead after suffering a heart attack.

Zoë found help in her practice while she was embroiled in her family's affairs by employing Paddy Kirk, who arrived in 1997 and fell for the ample charms of Mandy Dingle. Later, he returned permanently to the practice and, early in 1998, moved in with Mandy at Wishing Well Cottage. However, Paddy's good nature almost cost him his job when he treated ailing farmer Jed Outhwaite's animals for free.

After the tragic death of receptionist Linda Fowler, Zoë also found a new receptionist in Becky Cairns. When she started to drift apart from her husband, Tony, Becky sought a relationship with Zoë. Her son, Will, saw Becky kissing the vet and Tony walked out on his wife, heading for a new job in Germany. When Becky had to accept that Zoë was not interested in her, she left Emmerdale and joined her husband. Kelly Windsor was taken on as Zoë's new receptionist and, for a while, stayed at the cottage.

Zoë faces the wrath of ailing farmer Jed Outhwaite when she and vet Paddy Kirk arrive at his farm to treat his neglected animals.

The Woolpack

		Barmaids:	Alison Gibbons (1973)
1972–3	Amos Brearly		Dolly Acaster (later Skilbeck)
1973–91	Amos Brearly, Henry Wilks,		(1977–91)
	Dolly Acaster (1977)		Doreen Shuttleworth (1985)
1991–	Alan Turner, Carol Nelson		Meg Armstrong (1986)
	(1991–3), Shirley Foster (later		Kathy Merrick (1988)
	Turner) (1993–4), Terry Woods		Sarah Connolly (1990–1)
	(1995–), Britt Woods (1995),		Caroline Bates (1991)
	Tina Dingle (1995),		Elizabeth Feldmann (1991)
	Viv Windsor (1996–7),		Carol Nelson (1991–3)
	Donna Windsor (1996–7)		Rachel Hughes (1992, 1993)

Temporary managers: Caroline and Kathy Bates
(1987)

Guests: Asta and Olof Gunnarson (1977),
Archie Brooks (1987),
Jack Sugden, Sarah Connolly
and Robert Sugden (1993)

Shirley Foster (1993–4)
Jan Glover (1994–6)
Susie Wilde (1996)
Mandy Dingle (1997–8)
Heather Hutchinson (1998)

CREATING REALITY

The Woolpack began life as an exterior location in the Upper Dales village of Arncliffe, where outdoor filming was done for almost four years. In reality, it was the Falcon Inn, where the cast and crew stayed overnight while on location shooting.

When *Emmerdale* switched locations in 1976 to Esholt, closer to the Yorkshire Television studios, the village's Commercial Inn was used. Eventually, the landlord changed the real name to The Woolpack as tourists converged on the village.

The move to Harewood marked the pub's third location. Major changes to the building included new signs, a black front door and sliding sash windows.

'The building is far more imposing than the one at Esholt,' says designer Mike Long. 'I've changed the proportions of it, making it a little bit wider but not as high. It's now much more squat.

'Also, at Esholt, the door opened out onto the steep area in front of the pub, which I always thought was very odd. I've based the new door on that on a pub in Malham, in North Yorkshire. I also decided to make a much bigger tarmac area outside but keep it flatter. It was always very awkward at Esholt when we put pub tables outside – we had to build up one end of them on bricks.

'There is a hatch at the front of The Woolpack opening into a beer cellar so that we can show scenes of beer being delivered, but the cellar doesn't go all the way under the building.' There is also now a beer garden at the rear of the pub, plus a car park. 'We had a car park at Esholt,' says Mike, 'but we could rarely show it because that's where we kept our equipment vehicles.'

Although the inside of the new pub building at Harewood is mostly a shell, public lobbies have been built at front and back – including toilet doors – as well as a lobby and staircase at the rear leading to Alan Turner and Terry Woods's private accommodation, plus another door for them to use as an exit. This is visible in scenes of them using the stairs or going through the back door.

Net curtains no longer go all the way up the windows at the front of the pub. The studio set matches this and allows viewers to see a backcloth of the cottages opposite when looking out of the windows. Filming from outside on the Harewood set, especially at night when lights are on, gives the impression of a bustling pub inside, over the top of the curtains.

The studio set has had a number of changes to its design and décor over the years. 'The pub interior is used so much,' says Mike. 'It started off as a dark, chocolate brown. Then, a few years ago, Emma Nightingale redesigned the pub. As a result, we ended up with a compromise to suit the lighting directors. Whereas I wanted it darker and more atmospheric, the lighting people wanted it a bit lighter. I wasn't responsible for the wallpaper, but one of the things I noticed after it was put up was that it's exactly the same as that in the pub in EastEnders!'

The pub's small back room in the studio set is reached through a door behind the bar. 'When it was originally designed,' says Mike, 'they did quite flashy meals in a kitchen that was alluded to but doesn't exist.'

Henry Wilks and Amos Brearly team up at The Woolpack to become hosts to the regulars for almost 20 years.

Amos Seeks a Wife

Bachelor Amos, a former Royal Artillery member whose dour manner and pernickety ways were a trademark of The Woolpack's hospitality, took on Alison Gibbons as a barmaid in February 1973 when she arrived from Liverpool after the death of her husband and young son in a car crash – and a spell in prison for shoplifting.

The Revd Edward Ruskin, who had known Alison in Liverpool, invited her to the village because she had been very ill following the accident, for which she blamed herself, and was in need of a complete change. However, she left The Woolpack after turning down Amos's proposal of marriage, although she later returned to Beckindale to work at the village shop.

Double-act Behind the Bar

Amos found a companion at the pub in October 1973 after Henry Wilks suffered the loss of his house, Inglebrook, in a blaze. Widower Henry, a successful Bradford wool merchant, had moved to Beckindale the previous year with his daughter, Marian, after taking early retirement. Following the fire, Henry lodged temporarily at Emmerdale Farm before renting a room from Amos.

His stay was intended to be an interim measure, but that changed when the brewery, Skipdale-based Ephraim Monk's, decided to put the pub up for sale. Amos was devastated, but Henry came to the rescue, as he had done at the farm, by offering to buy it in partnership with Amos. As a result, the pair had a home *and* business in The Woolpack. For Henry, whose daughter had left earlier that year following a romance with Jack Sugden, Amos and the pub also guaranteed him some company.

Henry had to fight to get his ideas accepted by Amos, who was set in his ways after running the pub since 1948. But, whatever battles he faced with Amos, Henry was respected throughout the village.

The Woolpack, an 18th-century pub dating back to the days when wool was taken over the moors by packhorse during the Industrial Revolution, was the scene of a wake in the Yorkshire Dales village of Beckindale in 1972. After Annie Sugden had buried her farmer husband Jacob at St Mary's Church, she brought her family to The Woolpack for the funeral tea.

With her father, Sam Pearson, and younger son, Joe, as well as daughter Peggy and son-in-law Matt Skilbeck, sombre Annie contemplated life on Emmerdale Farm without her husband. Then elder son Jack came through the door, returning to the fold after eight years in London. The family was complete at a time of great sadness.

The Woolpack provided a focal point for villagers to congregate, much preferred by locals to the rival Malt Shovel, and irascible landlord Amos Brearly – noted for his bushy sideburns – could be relied on to ensure that the pub known by the community for decades would not be changed to adhere to so-called progress.

As well as putting money into Emmerdale Farm, he bought the village shop, served as both a church warden and parish councillor, and acted in many plays in the village hall. Ornithologist Henry combined the industrialist's vision he brought to the village with a concern for conservation, leaving the Dales as they were for future generations to benefit.

Annie's Refusal

Amos, who came from a family of undertakers on the Yorkshire coast, had come close to marrying after the Second World War but was jilted by his fiancée in favour of a local butcher. When, in 1973, it was suggested to Amos that his pub lacked a woman's touch, he decided this time to propose to Annie Sugden.

With no other likely targets, Amos thought that Annie must be lonely following the death of her husband and that he himself was a good catch, a clean-living man with a thriving business. Unfortunately, Annie did not agree with him and turned down his generous offer.

Close to Home

When, in 1976, farmer Tad Ryland's wife, Bella, suffered a long illness that ended in her death, Henry fell out with Amos, who had repeated to him the rumour that Tad subsequently planned to marry Nan Wheeler, who had nursed her cousin, Bella, and was a friend of Annie Sugden.

Henry usually took Amos's gossip in his stride, but this time it struck too close to home. Henry's own wife had died after a long illness, during which she was looked after by a nurse, and Nan had been a friend to Henry, giving him tips on pruning his roses. It was a few days before the Woolpack hosts were back on speaking terms.

Pub Crawls

Tragedy also struck in 1976 when subsidence caused the closure of The Woolpack. The problem emerged when a crack appeared in the fireplace wall. Fortunately, Amos and Henry were able to find premises in a more central position in the village at a former corn chandler's dwelling, built in the Victorian era.

However, when Amos heard that the pub was reputed to be haunted, he considered backing out of the purchase. Level-headed Henry eventually persuaded him not to listen to gossip, the move went ahead and they had the premises converted into a two-bar establishment retaining the 'olde worlde' charm of the original. The first Woolpack was sold and became a private house.

In the same year, Amos found another way of keeping at the centre of local gossip by becoming part-time Beckindale correspondent for the *Hotten Courier* newspaper following the death of Percy Edgar, who had previously contributed news items.

Amos takes time to adjust to having a woman, Dolly Acaster, working behind the bar.

Dolly Drops In

With Amos spending some time out and about on his bicycle gathering news for the local paper, Henry suggested hiring a live-in barmaid. As a result, Dolly Acaster arrived from Darlington on a brewery training scheme in February 1977.

Dolly's arrival unnerved Amos, who had doubts about employing a woman behind the bar. He addressed her as 'Miss Acaster', showed himself to be unco-operative and was put out that she went down so well with the regulars. Her experience as a set designer also enabled Dolly to help with a village concert. However, subjected to Amos's constant criticism, Dolly left to run a pub in Leeds.

When, later in the year, Amos – who rarely bowed to pressure for change – yielded to local demands to install real ale on tap in The Woolpack, he set about his research by going on a guided tour at Ephraim Monk's and found himself being shown round by Dolly, who had moved on from her pub job to work at the brewery.

Henry then re-employed Dolly, giving her accommodation above the pub, and Amos grew to like her. Dolly herself found romance with farm labourer Matt Skilbeck, whose wife Peggy – daughter of Annie Sugden – had died tragically four years earlier.

Bed and Breakfast

When The Woolpack started taking in bed-and-breakfast guests in 1977, Swedish visitors Asta and Olof Gunnarson stayed there. There was drama when they went pot-holing and were trapped in Baker's Pot. Fortunately, the Wharfedale Rescue Team, including Matt Skilbeck, pulled them to safety.

During the year, Henry met old flame Janet Thompson when he visited a nearby Dales village called Littlewell. It appeared that they might re-ignite the romance from the days before his marriage, but it never happened.

Pub Under Threat

It was a terrifying ordeal for Amos and Henry when, in 1978, teenagers Steve Hawker and Pip Coulter robbed The Woolpack and locked them in the cellar overnight. The robbers then headed for Emmerdale Farm, where they held Sam Pearson at gunpoint. His daughter, Annie Sugden, saved the day by providing the pair with a getaway car.

Later in the year, Amos moved out of the pub to recuperate at Emmerdale Farm after contracting chickenpox from Seth Armstrong's son, Fred. During his absence, Henry's daughter, Marian, arrived from Italy and tried to persuade her father to move there. Henry contemplated selling his share in The Woolpack to an old Army officer friend, Major Denyer, but eventually decided against it and the partnership with Amos continued.

But it was under threat again the following year, when Henry fell for widow Irene Madden, who had moved in next to Joe Sugden in Demdyke Row. As with Janet Thompson before her, the friendship with Henry did not turn to romance and Amos was relieved.

Amos himself was under threat when the *Hotten Courier*'s editor wanted to replace him with Frank Hencoller in 1981, the year in which Henry was elected a parish councillor. In the event, Amos was made redundant but then reinstated.

The Bishop and the Ferret

One of The Woolpack's most regular customers down the years has been Seth Armstrong, whose poaching activities were curtailed when he became NY Estates' gamekeeper in 1979. Three years later, Amos barred Seth from the pub when he introduced the Bishop of Hotten to his pet ferret.

The Donkey and the Bees

In 1985, Amos infuriated NY Estates manager Alan Turner by supplying the *Hotten Courier* with a front-page article about children being hospitalised after wind carried chemicals that had been sprayed on Home Farm land.

The piece was published on the day of the village fête, when Alan parked the NY show caravan on the forecourt of The Woolpack and threatened Amos with legal action for libel. But locals rounded on him and were joined by Seth

Armstrong's donkey, which ran off after giving rides to children.

After pushing Alan into his van and leaving a mess on the caravan floor, the donkey upset a beehive, with the result that a swarm of bees chased Amos down the village street until he threw himself into the pond – not realising that, by then, the bees had already stopped off at a tree.

Extra help was at hand in The Woolpack on the day of the fête in the shape of Malt Shovel barmaid Doreen. She was hired in the absence of Henry, who was visiting daughter Marian in Italy.

Amos's Antiques

In the course of writing another article for the *Hotten Courier*, Amos attended local auctions and began to show an interest in collecting antiques. He had already accumulated many items over the years, including a dancing bear coat stand, a pianola that did not work and, following the death of an uncle, a pair of elephant's feet umbrella stands that he inherited. Now, Amos began to buy all sorts of paraphernalia, such as clocks and a phrenologist's head. Soon, there was no room for any more at The Woolpack and Henry called a halt to it.

So, when Amos continued with his buying addiction, he stored the articles in a barn at Emmerdale Farm. Then Annie Sugden gave Sandie Merrick and Phil Pearce permission to take some furniture stored there to furnish their new home at The Mill and they ended up removing Amos's belongings. On a visit there with Henry, Amos spotted the items but was unable to complain because that would have revealed his ruse.

Bars and Brawls

Like many pubs, The Woolpack has been the venue of several brawls and confrontations down the years. When, in 1986, builder Phil Pearce had an affair with auctioneer Sandie Merrick, Phil's wife, Lesley, had a showdown with her husband's lover in the pub, accusing her of being a tart and stealing her husband.

In 1993, two women were at the centre of the action again when Rachel Hughes doused Lynn

Lynn Whiteley accepts a free gin-and-tonic from barmaid Rachel Hughes, who once had an affair with her late husband, Pete.

Whiteley with a gin-and-tonic in front of a crowded Woolpack after hearing about her stepfather Joe's relationship with her old rival.

The previous year, Michael Feldmann felled Eric Pollard in the pub when he disapproved of his mother Elizabeth's romance with the dodgy dealer, but it was not enough to stop the couple marrying. It did, however, result in Michael being barred.

Politics in the Pub

The Woolpack was the venue for a second public meeting when, in 1987, villagers protested against plans by the government to site an underground nuclear waste dump at nearby Pencross Fell. A campaign of action subsequently resulted in the proposals being abandoned.

Doting Grandfather

In the same year, Henry Wilks was pleased to see his daughter, Marian, return to Beckindale from Italy with husband Paolo Rossetti and his newborn grandson, Niccolo. Marian's old flame, Jack Sugden, was also pleased to see her and took advantage of the situation when Paolo ended up in hospital in a coma.

Staying at Thornpark, rented for him and Marian by Henry, Paolo accidentally shot himself as he chased Eric Pollard, who was trying to burgle the house. Paolo emerged from hospital confined to a wheelchair for life, Marian's fling ended and the couple returned to Italy.

Another notable event at The Woolpack in 1987 was Amos and Henry taking a holiday together, leaving Caroline Bates and her daughter, Kathy, in charge.

Dicing with Death

Rumours of The Woolpack being haunted resurfaced in 1990 when a Dales tourism brochure's typographical mistake credited the pub with a 'welcoming ghost' instead of a 'welcoming host'. But Amos did not complain when believers in the supernatural flocked to the pub.

More worrying for Amos during the year was when, in November, he was forgotten and left trapped in the cellar after a chemical tanker crashed into a wall in Main Street, outside the pub, and everyone was evacuated from the area. Henry locked the cellar door, presuming that his partner had left. Fortunately, Frank Tate came to the rescue and led Amos to safety.

He came even closer to death after suffering a stroke at Annie Sugden's seventieth-birthday party celebrations in The Woolpack. It was an ominous sign, which made Amos begin to think about his future.

During 1990, the pub also took on a new barmaid, when Jack Sugden's girlfriend, Sarah Connolly, started pulling pints after budget cuts resulted in her job in the mobile library being axed. However, she eventually left to work with Jack on the farm.

End of an Era

After 43 years as landlord of The Woolpack, Amos decided to retire to Spain in 1991 following his stroke the previous year. Momentous changes were to come as Alan Turner, former NY Estates manager who had more recently run the fish and game farm, bought the pub on 30 January and Henry Wilks stayed on to help during the transition. It was a great loss to the village when Henry died of a heart attack on 3 October 1991.

Turner Takes His Turn

Alan immediately set about changing Beckindale's most popular hostelry, which irritated Henry during his last months in The Woolpack – and some of the regulars. In March 1991, when the brewery, Ephraim Monk's, was unable to supply beer while new pipes were being fitted, Alan switched to the rival Skipdale Brewery.

It seemed to be characteristic of the new landlord that the work should be followed by a grand

After buying The Woolpack in 1991, Alan Turner intends to put his stamp on it by introducing gourmet meals in a restaurant situated in the old tap-room.

reopening that was attended by the scantily clad Miss Skipdale Breweries. But Alan had reckoned without his customers, and Seth Armstrong complained about the quality of the new ale and led a walkout that forced Alan to switch back to Ephraim Monk's.

However, this was not to deter Alan from turning the old tap-room into a restaurant that would offer gourmet cooking and, he hoped, attract an exclusive clientele. The new landlord even advertised on local radio in an attempt to attract the up-market custom for which he aimed.

In September, after employing Caroline Bates and Elizabeth Feldmann as part-time bar staff, Alan took on Carol Nelson as a full-time barmaid. At the centre of the village's social activity, she soon became a purveyor of the latest gossip.

Food for Thought

Locals proved slow in flocking to eat Alan's *haute cuisine*. When he took a break at a health farm, Carol changed the menu to offer diners such homely foods as steak-and-kidney pie and traditional roast beef and Yorkshire pudding. Although this resulted in takings going up, Alan on his return could not let such down-market dishes take over the menu.

When he appointed Lynn Whiteley *maîtresse d'*, she suggested that the dishes should be more suited to the budgets of people arriving from the Holiday Village. Alan agreed to give her a 60/40 share in the increased profits that resulted but staunchly rebuffed Lynn's attempts to persuade him that the restaurant should be switched back to a bar serving home cooking and fast food, with children allowed in and the gourmet night abandoned.

However, he was eventually forced to rethink his position as holidaymakers shunned his highly priced posh meals. A salmonella scare also gave Alan time to reconsider his position, although a health inspector eventually cleared his suspected jam-filled omelette dessert of being responsible for the scare.

He gave Lynn *carte blanche* to organise the restaurant the way she felt fit. She transformed it into a popular wine bar and such was the increased custom that she found help in the shape of Carol's headstrong daughter, Lorraine, who also moved in with her at Whiteley's Farm.

Game, Seth and Match

At about the same time, the Home Farm estate's fish and game farm was split up, with Frank Tate taking over the fish farm and Alan keeping his interest in the game reserve. As part of the deal, Alan demanded that both gamekeeper Seth Armstrong and his fish farm manager, Elizabeth Feldmann, should not lose their jobs. Although he disapproved of Elizabeth's romance with slimy Eric Pollard, Alan agreed to act as chief usher at their wedding.

Christmas Cheer

For his first Christmas at The Woolpack, Alan was determined to score points against the rival Malt Shovel, and long-serving landlord Ernie Shuttleworth, by providing a pensioners' turkey dinner on Christmas Day. Seth arranged for 17 pensioners to attend, but Alan wondered what was happening when they all briskly ate their free meal and, at the clap of Seth's hands, hurriedly left without eating their plum pudding. Seth informed him that they were all off to The Malt Shovel for Ernie's seasonal gesture of goodwill.

Alan marked his first year in charge at The Woolpack with a fancy-dress party based on historic events and characters on 30 January. The landlord's own first choice of costume, as Oliver Hardy – who had been born 100 years earlier – was abandoned after local wags dubbed him 'Hitler's second cousin', 'Charlie Chaplin' and 'Fatty Arbuckle'. Alan eventually settled on Charles II, remarking to barmaid Carol that it was a pity men no longer dressed so boldly.

The party was a great success, with Seth Armstrong and Bill Middleton arriving as the Wright brothers – Bill speaking like a duck and claiming to be Orville Wright – Frank Tate as Charles I, Archie Brooks as Mahatma Gandhi and Kim Tate as an Indian temptress.

Barmaid as Mother

Barmaid Carol showed a magic touch when she laid her healing hands on Jack Sugden after he had been assaulted by thugs trying to break into Mark Hughes's cottage and was suffering pain. But Carol had problems of her own with tearaway teenage daughter Lorraine, who found a job at Frank Tate's Holiday Village in 1992 but was eventually sacked.

Carol – herself sacked from The Woolpack by Alan for gossiping and apparently reporting single father Nick Bates and his childminder friend, Archie Brooks, to social services – tried to get to the root of her daughter's problems and discovered that her ex-husband, Derek, had until recently been abusing Lorraine.

This sent Carol into a depression and Alan proved uncharacteristically understanding, offering the barmaid her job back despite opposition from some regulars. The following year, when Lorraine landed a place at art college, Carol left Beckindale to be closer to her.

For the first time in years, Alan loosens up as Shirley Foster brings love into his life, although it is tragically to be taken away from him after their marriage.

A New Alan

When Caroline Bates, Alan's former fiancée, returned to Beckindale from Scarborough in 1993, he tried to resume their romance. He proposed once more, but she turned him down. Assuring Alan of her loyal friendship, Caroline suggested that he should socialise more in an attempt to meet eligible women.

As a result, she took him to a tea-dance, then a drop-in centre, where he met Shirley Foster as he donned an apron and ladled out soup to the homeless and down-and-outs in the soup kitchen, a humbling experience for a man who in the past would have looked down on such people in society.

Shirley found him to be an 'arrogant pig', but Alan was genuinely touched by the news that the body of a young woman called Tina who had visited

the centre was later found in a barn, where she had died of natural causes. Coming to realise he had seen little of the world around him, nor cared about it, Alan even spent a night living rough on the streets. This brought him closer to Shirley and he began to put aside his aloofness and allowed himself to live a little and enjoy himself.

However, it took much more for Alan to come to terms with the discovery that Shirley had once been a prostitute, whose morals had fallen way below those befitting his own apparently high social status. He even observed a group of young women calling at her home and assumed they made money by selling their bodies, but Shirley explained that they came to her for counselling.

Realising how much Shirley meant to him and how much she had changed his life, Alan ate humble pie and told her that he wanted to continue their relationship because life with her meant more to him than his previous high-flown principles. When Carol Nelson left The Woolpack, Shirley took over as barmaid following the closure of the drop-in centre.

When a plane crashes over Beckindale in 1993, The Woolpack's windows are blown in by an explosion and the wine bar is devastated.

Tragedy Strikes

Kathy Tate, who stepped in to help Lynn Whiteley in running the wine bar, found new romance with American wine salesman Josh Lewis as her marriage to husband Chris crumbled. The pair plotted to leave Beckindale together but, on the night they had arranged to leave, 30 December 1993, their plans were undone by the plane disaster that rocked Beckindale.

Alan had arranged a Dickensian Evening to raise money for Seth Armstrong's prostate operation. However, as events got under way, with the genial pub landlord dressed as Mr Pickwick, an ungrateful Seth complained about the poor attendance and was barred by Alan. Leaving The Woolpack, he threatened to take his custom to The Malt Shovel.

Shortly afterwards, the revelry was brought to an abrupt end as an explosion shattered the pub's windows and devastated the wine bar. Alan, Shirley and their customers crashed to the ground. As villagers came to grips with what had happened, a rescue operation was mounted to save those who had not perished.

Seth was missing, presumed dead, after it was discovered that his house in Demdyke Row had been destroyed. Alan was overcome with emotion at the thought that he had sent his old sparring partner to his death. So it was with relief, and tears welling in his eyes, that he greeted Seth later as the infuriating gamekeeper walked back into the village with Samson the stallion, having found safety with widow Betty Eagleton during the horrors.

Another survivor was found when Josh Lewis heard a cry for help from under the rubble of the wine bar. On moving some of the débris, he discovered it was Kathy's husband, Chris. Kathy held his hand as he was dug out of the rubble, with the help of Samson the horse, later to discover that he was paralysed and confined to a wheelchair for life. When Kathy's eyes met those of her lover, Josh knew that their dreams were not to be. He broke into her cottage and removed the goodbye letter that she had left for Chris.

Back From the Brink

Life was turned on its head in Beckindale by the disaster, and the discovery of a thousand-year-old corpse among the rubble of The Woolpack was not good news for trade as Alan set about refurbishing the pub, with Shirley at his side to help.

He was happier when archaeologists established that the human remains were those of a Viking and was able to reopen The Woolpack as a theme pub with a Viking artefact. A group of musicians recommended by Luke McAllister and Biff Fowler arrived in evening dress to provide entertainment befitting the tone that Alan had set for the establishment, only to break out into a raucous sound of heavy metal. With the group swiftly unplugged, and pranksters Luke and Biff barred, Seth sat down at the recently acquired pianola to lead a more appropriate, old-fashioned singalong.

However, Alan faced competition from not just The Malt Shovel but also Frank Tate and Lynn Whiteley's newly opened country club and the off-licence established by Vic and Viv Windsor at the village stores.

Short-lived Happiness

Shirley brought new meaning to Alan's life and the couple married at Hotten Register Office on 10 February 1994, with a pony and trap taking them to and from the ceremony. Warm-hearted Shirley proved to be a calming influence on Alan, who visibly mellowed and became a more genial host at The Woolpack.

The pub landlord could not believe how lucky he was to have found such a caring person. So he was heartbroken when his new wife was shot dead in the aftermath of a raid at the village post office only four months after the wedding. Alan himself was wounded by a stray bullet in a shoot-out at The Woolpack after the raiders had left the post office with Viv Windsor as hostage and grabbed Shirley, using her Range Rover as a get-away vehicle.

Viv and Shirley were taken to a deserted Home Farm, where the leader of the gang – Viv's ex-husband, Reg Dawson – accidentally shot one of his accomplices, then aimed for Viv. It was typical of Shirley that she intervened to save the village postmistress and gave her own life in doing so. Police marksmen storming the house then shot Reg dead.

A Broken Man

On his return home from hospital, grief-stricken Alan was a broken man. Aware that Viv Windsor had previously looked down on Shirley as a common tart, he was in no mood to hear the eulogies that she now heaped on his dead wife. Alan banned Viv and husband Vic from Shirley's funeral but eventually changed his mind, realising that he had to adopt a positive approach as he faced a future without the one woman who had brought joy into his life.

However, sinking to his lowest point, Alan hit the whisky bottle and resumed his gambling ways of old. Shady Eric Pollard appeared to offer comfort, but it soon became apparent that he was simply an opportunist hoping to cash in on Alan's misfortune.

As the pub landlord hit rock bottom, not even able to perform behind the wicket in the village cricket match against Robblesfield, and with the VAT man knocking at the door, Pollard persuaded Alan to allow him to examine The Woolpack's finances in an effort to help him out of the mire.

In the event, Pollard concocted tales of Shirley keeping false accounts, painted a dire picture of the situation at the pub and suggested that they set up a brewery producing the exclusive Emmerd Ale. He tried to persuade Alan to take a £20,000 loan from him with The Woolpack as security, but the publican recovered his senses in time to prevent his own, final descent.

Bar managers Terry and Britt Woods bring a breath of fresh air with their arrival in 1995, but Britt's past catches up with her and leads to her walking out on her husband.

Life Goes On

Facing the future, Alan decided to give The Woolpack a facelift and hired interior designer Emma Nightingale to come up with a new look. Emma later fell for lesbian vet Zoë Tate, and Alan introduced new faces at the pub in the form of Terry and Britt Woods. This came about after he asked the brewery, Ephraim Monk's, for financial help with the redesign and it responded with the view that it would look more favourably at the request if Alan appointed a manager.

Terry and Britt, who had run a bar in Benidorm, jointly filled this job, although Alan made it clear that he was still the boss and running the business. A reopening ceremony took place in February 1995 with cricketer Ian Botham cutting the red ribbon and drawing the raffle, whose first prize of a free meal for the family was won by Nellie Dingle.

Returning the following evening with 12 of the terrible Dingles in tow, she pointed out that there had been no mention of a restriction on numbers. When Alan presented the family with a drinks bill, they paid in 10p pieces stolen from their gas meter. Although the benefit of their presence in the pub was dubious, the Dingle clan subsequently became regulars there.

During the course of the refurbishment, Alan threw out the pub's old bar furniture and the Woolpack well, which found its way to the Dingles' dilapidated farm buildings, where Zak presented it as a Valentine's Day gift to wife Nellie.

Terrible Terry

Terry Woods soon landed in trouble when he bought Seth Armstrong and Vic Windsor's home-made moonshine whisky to sell at the pub. Then, claiming that he could get it cheaper elsewhere, he cancelled the order. Seth and Vic were convinced that Terry could not buy it for less and mounted a surveillance operation that proved that their drink was being stolen and finding its way to The Woolpack.

As a result, Alan threatened to sack Terry, but Britt suggested that she should become manageress with sole responsibility behind the bar. This left Terry as little more than a general dogsbody, collecting glasses and looking after the cellar. Soon, the marriage came under strain.

Britt's Dark Secret

There was further pressure on Britt when her father, Ronnie Slater, arrived. This was a particular surprise to husband Terry because he had believed Britt's father to be dead. It emerged that Ronnie had abused Britt as a child. Although Ronnie eventually agreed to leave, this revelation left a strain on Britt's marriage and she became more distant from Terry.

Given the chance of a new start by managing the brewery's flagship pub in York, Britt believed this could save the marriage. Terry felt that it was simply running away from the problem and refused to go. So Britt left for York on her own and Terry stayed at The Woolpack as manager.

Although Terry found romance with Tina Dingle – who moved into the pub for a while – and *Hotten Courier* reporter Helen Ackroyd, he made a Christmas attempt at reconciliation with Britt. He visited her in York, only to find that she had taken up with brewery representative Gerald Taylor.

Terry's Mistress

After later discovering he had a son by a former girlfriend and that Britt was pregnant with Gerald's child, Terry tried to rekindle the flames with Tina Dingle. She showed little interest, but new love came into Terry's life when he began an affair with postmistress Viv Windsor, who cheated on her husband, Vic, after starting dancing classes with Terry at the village hall.

When Viv's son, Scott, travelled to Catterick for his first day in the Army in September 1996, Viv went with him and met Terry at a nearby hotel afterwards. Later, Vic walked in on Viv and Terry together in the back room at the post office. Once their affair had been discovered, Viv moved in with Terry at the pub.

However, proving that Viv had been caught on the rebound following Terry's unhappy marital split, he dumped her by claiming that he had fallen

for *Hotten Courier* reporter Helen Ackroyd. In fact, they had enjoyed a one-night stand and this was the only excuse he could muster for letting Viv down.

Staff Matters

Someone else going through a bad period was Jan Glover, who had started work behind the bar at The Woolpack in 1994, after Shirley's death. Two years later, she was sacked by Alan when he found her dipping into the till in an effort to pay off her debts. Alan later found a new barmaid in buxom Mandy Dingle and sacked Terry in 1997 after he had allowed Donna Windsor – daughter of his then girlfriend, Viv – to drink unsupervised in The Woolpack.

Terry then worked as a barman at Pollard's Wine Bar and lodged with Betty Eagleton and Seth Armstrong. But after Alan broke his leg when some barrels fell on it and Terry helped out, the landlord invited his former employee to return as bar manager – with the added incentive of ten per cent of the profits.

For a short time, Mandy moved into The Wool-pack when her Uncle Albert contracted mumps, but Alan and Terry – proving to be a partnership in the tradition of Amos Brearly and Henry Wilks – engineered her departure by constantly leaving the place in a mess.

Alan found romance again with biker Jo Steadman, but she left for America after failing to persuade him to join her, and Terry subsequently had a fling with Heather Hutchinson, who was working as a barmaid.

Once more, love comes and goes in Alan's life with the arrival of biker Jo Steadman.

Pubs and Pints

Richard Thorp, who plays pub landlord Alan Turner, was on hand to represent *Emmerdale's* Woolpack when the Yorkshire Brewers' Association arranged a get-together of all licensees of Woolpack pubs in Yorkshire and Humberside during British Pub Week in 1993.

Twelve publicans joined Richard for the special occasion at The Woolpack in Esholt, near Bradford, where the exterior of the TV pub was then filmed. The group included Bryan Hirst of the real-life pub in Esholt, which was called The Commercial Inn until he changed its name following an influx of tourists.

But those coming to see the *Emmerdale* pub did not find what they expected. 'Members of the public used to come and see the outside of the pub,' says Richard, 'then they would go marching in through the front door and think they'd come to the wrong place because the inside was totally different from what we had in the studio.'

Richard points out that the Woolpack regulars who drink beer during interior scenes in the studio get the best deal. 'Anyone who drinks beer is on a much better bet than those who drink whisky, gin, vodka or sherry because they get the real thing, whereas the others get coloured water,' he reveals.

The actor is also a stickler for realism when it comes to pulling pints. 'We're much more strict about that than the other soaps are,' says Richard. 'They often pull a pint from under the counter and pop it on the bar.

'I'm a bloody nuisance to most of the programme directors – as were Ronald Magill and Arthur Pentelow before me, playing Amos and Henry – because I say that if I'm serving a drink I cannot serve it in that length of time and be paid and get the change. I hate the thing of people giving me ready money rather than waiting for their change.'

Pear Tree Cottage

| 1996– | Steve Marchant, Faye Clarke (1996), |
| | Kim Marchant (1998–), James Tate (1998–) |

CREATING REALITY

Steve and Kim Marchant's small cottage, previously a location in Esholt, is used for filming exteriors and scenes in the porch. The new outdoor set also allowed designer Mike Long to give the then single Steve a rear garden with barbecue.

In reality, the ground floor of Pear Tree Cottage – next to The Woolpack and at the end of a terrace of four – houses male and female changing rooms, plus a costume office, and the first floor is the Green Room, where actors and actresses can relax between scenes.

There is access from upstairs to the ground floor of the house next door, Woodbine Cottage, where *Emmerdale*'s make-up artists are based.

Like other houses on the set at Harewood, the windows in this cottage have plaster around them on the inside and a deep reveal so that views can be filmed out of them.

The open-plan studio set was designed by Mike Long, who had the chance to inject a slightly yuppi-fied feel to reflect Steve's use of computers and other technology in his work as a financial consultant.

'Steve was a computer whiz-kid and quite a wealthy man when he moved in, so we made the room as smart as possible,' says Mike. 'We chose all the props to make it look a bit more masculine – such as the buffalo-grey sofa and muted colours – because at the time he was living by himself.

'But after his money crisis and marriage to Kim, Steve's computer, television, stereo and other gadgets were removed by Eric Pollard and the Dingles to recoup money for the wedding catering bill.'

Above *Financial whiz-kid Steve Marchant engineers girlfriend Faye Clarke's departure from Emmerdale.*

Top right *It is not long before Steve becomes close to his former university friend Rachel Tate after his move to the village.*

Right *Pear Tree Cottage is all that Steve and wife Kim have from their first day of marriage after the groom loses all their money in bad investments.*

Financial whiz-kid Steve Marchant brought new technology to the Dales when he bought Pear Tree Cottage, next door to The Woolpack, in August 1996. A former university friend of Rachel Tate, Steve set up as an independent financial consultant there and his girlfriend, Faye Clarke, moved in with him. But, with designs on Rachel, he manoeuvred Faye's departure by arranging a job for her in New York.

Seeking to jazz up Rachel's image, Steve took her shopping, bought her clothes and asked her to help run his business. Rachel was married to Chris Tate and had a baby son, Joseph. Although she had already walked out on her husband once, they were back together – but their days seemed numbered.

Quarrysome Businessman

However, before cementing his relationship with Rachel, Steve romanced Tina Dingle. He dumped her after one of his dodgy business dealings came to light – buying Emmerdale Farm land that he knew Chris Tate's father, Frank, was desperate to lay his hands on to give him an access road to a quarry. Steve hoped he would be able to make a killing by selling it on to the lord of the manor.

But Frank showed his greater experience by sitting back and letting Steve's loan-interest payments mount up until he was forced to sell the land for the same price he had bought it – and lost everything he had paid in interest.

Rachel, seeking a way out of being a downtrodden housewife and mother, had ironically been spurred on by the campaign against Frank's quarry plans. After she had taken part in protests, husband Chris ordered her to leave The Mill, although he later granted the house to her in a divorce settlement.

After Frank's Own Heart

Despite the rivalry over the Emmerdale Farm land deal, Frank Tate urged daughter Zoë to appoint Steve as acting company manager of Tate Holdings, responsible for its financial affairs, while Frank languished in prison on remand, charged with the murder of his wife, Kim. Steve subsequently bought 20 per cent of the company's shares.

Rachel was enraged to find out that Steve had not told Frank about husband Chris's debts of £400,000, because it would affect her divorce settlement. Then Rachel made a mistake that cost Steve's business thousands of pounds and, following an argument, she dumped him.

Boardroom to Bedroom

When Kim miraculously reappeared and Frank died, she saw Steve's potential in the boardroom *and* bedroom, and he became an important cog in her business empire. But Kim was keen to assert her independence and rejected Steve's advice when Lord Alex Oakwell, down on his luck, wanted her to become his business partner in a stud farm.

So, instead of using Tate Holdings to invest in it, she put in her own money – and made a play for the aristocrat. But Lord Oakwell married Tara Cockburn, who was interested only in his title. When Kim went away to New Zealand on business, Tara became friendly with Steve, and discovered that he was really called Trevor and grew up with a foster family in a terraced house after not really knowing his parents.

Steve also introduced Tara to his foster father, John Kenyon, who explained that he and his wife, Janey, had brought 'Trevor' up from the age of 11. Tara subsequently chastised Steve for being embarrassed about his past and called him a snob for distancing himself from his foster father. She delighted in the fact that she knew something about Steve that Kim did not.

For Richer or Poorer

By then, Steve had proposed to Kim. They married on 7 May 1998 but, as wedding guests saw them off for the honeymoon, the couple harboured the secret that both had lost their money and were on their uppers following the collapse of his business and the loss of her own money in trying to save it.

While Lady Tara Oakwell bought their controlling interest in Home Farm, Kim faced the prospect of life in Pear Tree Cottage and Steve took whatever work he could get to earn a living, in the hope that one day they would bounce back.

Dale Head Farm

Workshop
1998–   Lisa Dingle

CREATING REALITY

ale Head Farm, with its barn and workshop, was built on the Harewood outdoor set as one of half-a-dozen empty houses not allocated to *Emmerdale* characters when filming began there. It is at the far end of the terrace from Steve and Kim Marchant's cottage, with two others in between.

Designer Mike Long earmarked this cottage as his office. The barn, used for exterior shots only, actually houses the production team's electrical equipment, including smoke machines and controls for the street lighting and chimney smoke.

The workshop and yard, where Lisa Dingle bases her car-repair business, includes an inspection pit in the ground dating from its time as a garage. Previous producer Mervyn Watson asked for an old petrol pump to be included on the land – for a story in which Lisa's husband, Zak, sold diesel fuel with the result that cars broke down – as well as many rusty old artefacts to be littered around.

isa Dingle stumbled on her workshop when she and husband Zak were looking for somewhere to base her car-repair business. It is on the site of an old garage and, on opening the doors of the workshop in the spring of 1998, the couple discovered an old car covered in blankets. This proved to be the perfect base for Lisa, who had started the business outside Wishing Well Cottage after previously doing building work.

The Mill

1973–4	Jack Sugden, Trash (1973), Gwen Russell (1973)	1995–7	Chris Tate and Rachel Hughes, Joseph Hughes
1986–9	Phil Pearce and Sandie Merrick Kate Hughes, Rachel Hughes, Mark Hughes (all 1988–9)	1997– Lodgers:	Rachel Hughes, Joseph Hughes Annie Sugden (1993), Seth Armstrong (1994),
1989–90	Dolly Skilbeck, Sam Skilbeck		Nick Bates (1994),
1991–5	Chris and Kathy Tate		Alice Bates (1994)

CREATING REALITY

Rachel Hughes's house, first seen in early episodes of *Emmerdale* as a derelict watermill that Jack Sugden earmarked for conversion, presented designer Mike Long with the chance to upgrade the building previously used for outdoor filming into something more elegant. It has also been brought closer to the village.

'In Esholt, we never really got to grips with that as an exterior,' he says. 'There was no mill there, so we used a cottage, filmed the corner of it and never saw a wide shot. Rachel and her former husband, Chris Tate, were supposed to have had a bit of money, so I wanted to build something a bit more imposing.

'On the Harewood set, I've positioned it near the stream, on the edge of the village, looking back up the main street. I'd like to think that we might use it for interior shots in the future because it's very big inside – and space helps when filming interiors on location. Maybe Rachel could move out and it could be turned into a hotel, a doctor's surgery or an office.'

The original mill location, used in 1973 after Jack Sugden returned to the village from London, was filmed nearby at a building on the Harewood estate. 'I've based this on the original mill,' says Mike. 'Over the few years before building the village at Harewood, we used a small place in Esholt and the writers started calling it Mill Cottage in the story, which is wrong really because a mill is a big building.

'As a result, everyone thinks that what I've built at Harewood is wrong. But I've gone back to what it was originally – a mill next to a stream, and the biggest building on the Harewood site.

'It's built out of coursed sandstone, slightly different from all the other buildings, with sliding sash windows. The track next to The Mill goes down to a ford, which we created across the stream. There's quite a lot of planting around it that will grow into a woodland so that the house will eventually be surrounded by trees.'

When the Emmerdale Production Centre moved from Farsley to Leeds, Mike increased the size of the studio set in accordance with his plans at Harewood. 'I extended the kitchen, which had previously been no more than a galley,' he says. 'I also extended the sitting room by about six feet and moved the staircase. From that room you can see the lobby and front door, which matches the outdoor set.'

Following the death of tramp Trash, Jack Sugden is visited by his daughter, Penny Golightly (left), and gives accommodation to Gwen Russell, girlfriend of David Rhys.

the same time, he tipped off the *Hotten Courier* newspaper that Dale Properties, of which Verney was a major shareholder, was threatening to evict blacksmith Frank Blakey from the Beckindale Forge, wrongly assuming that Verney was behind the move.

The squire's discovery of this led him to give Jack a public whipping with his hunting crop in the courtyard of The Woolpack. Accepting his mistake, Jack did not seek to protect himself. The Verneys' marriage ended shortly afterwards.

Trash Drops In – and Out

Jack had found a new companion in the form of a tramp known as Trash, whom he befriended and allowed to live in The Mill after finding him asleep on a newspaper in front of the fire. His real name was Ian McIntyre and he had once been a librarian with a wife and daughter, but his reluctance to conform led him to leave home and live rough.

Trash was often seen at the Beckindale Sheepdog Trials and, during those in January 1973, witnessed Jim Latimer ensnaring 17-year-old Sharon Crossthwaite in the ruins of a nearby abbey. Latimer chased him off before returning to rape and murder the girl.

Having an aversion to the police, Trash said nothing, but as the search went on for Sharon's body he handed Jack the watch that she had been wearing. Jack persuaded him to tell PC Ball, the village bobby, but returned to The Mill after a trip to London with Laura Verney to discover that Trash had committed suicide by jumping out of a first-floor window and breaking his neck.

Trash's daughter, Penny Golightly, subsequently visited Beckindale and Gwen Russell, girlfriend of Emmerdale Farm labourer David Rhys, stayed at The Mill for a while.

Jack became increasingly isolated in The Mill and, in January 1974, feeling that his return to Dales life had proved fruitless, left for Rome to work

A derelict 19th-century watermill on Emmerdale Farm's land, ripe for conversion, seemed an ideal home for Jack Sugden on his return to Beckindale in 1972 after the death of his father, Jacob. The following year, after staying with mother Annie and his family in the farmhouse, Jack became the tenant at The Mill, which brought back to him magical childhood memories. He saw it as a place of solitude where he could combine farm work with his literary ambitions, following success in London as the author of a best-selling novel, *The Field of Tares*.

Although a friend, Bart Ansett, arrived from London to help with the conversion work, Jack soon gave up the idea of transforming The Mill and lived in it as it was. Distracted by the presence of Henry Wilks's daughter, Marian, he also found it difficult to get to grips with writing a second novel. However, their romance fizzled out after Jack refused to make a commitment to her, echoing the love story told in his successful novel, and she left for a Greek islands cruise before settling in New Zealand and, later, Italy.

Lord of the Manners?

When carefree Jack sought another woman, he made the mistake of launching into an affair with Laura, wife of lord of the manor George Verney. At

on a film script of his novel. Another attraction of the Italian capital was that Marian Wilks's travels had ended there.

Price of Conversion

The Mill was declared unsafe a year later and left uninhabited until it went up for auction in October 1986, when Jack – who had by then returned from Italy and made a new commitment to farming with his family – was outbid for it by brother Joe and builder Phil Pearce, who had just set up Phoenix Developments and intended to turn the building into two holiday flats.

Joe was furious that his brother's sentimental attempts to secure the property that had once been his home pushed the price up by £10,000, to £35,000, but it was perfect for the renovation work that Joe and Phil planned.

A Village Scandal

Phil himself moved into one of the unrenovated flats there in December 1986 with Hotten Market auctioneer Sandie Merrick, daughter of Jack's then wife, Pat, after leaving his own wife, Lesley, and spending a short time staying at 3 Demdyke Row with Joe. At least allowing the couple to use The Mill as their love-nest removed them from under Joe's feet, although their affair caused a scandal in Beckindale.

When they were looking to furnish The Mill, Annie Sugden agreed to let Sandie and Phil have some old family junk that had been stored in a barn on Emmerdale Farm. In looking for it, the couple happened on some antique items stored there secretly by Woolpack landlord Amos Brearly after his business partner, Henry Wilks, insisted that there was no room for more furniture at the pub. Not realising it was antique, Sandie and Phil considered the furniture to be awful but thought it would suffice until they could afford better.

The first Amos knew of this was when he and Henry visited the couple at The Mill. However, he was unable to say anything without giving away his secret to Henry, and he could not berate Sandie and Phil for taking items that he was not supposed to have bought.

Sandie Makes an Enemy

At work, Sandie fell foul of new head auctioneer Eric Pollard in 1987 after discovering that he had been fiddling the books and diverting antiques for his own private sale. She told Joe, who was regional manager of NY Estates, which had bought the market the previous year.

As a result, Pollard was sacked and mounted a hate campaign against Sandie, which culminated in him breaking into The Mill and drunkenly threatening her with a poker. Although Sandie was promoted to his job, that came to an abrupt end when NY Estates sold the market and pulled out of Beckindale altogether later in the year.

Sandie and Phil had planned to buy the mill conversion outright after Sandie made it clear that she did not want to lose the only home they had enjoyed together once the work was completed. But while Sandie put money aside, Phil simply hoped for a windfall that never came.

A day before the agreement was due to be signed, the couple had a huge row after Phil admitted that he could not find the money. Phil and Sandie's relationship ended, as did Phoenix Developments, which was wound up after NY Estates pulled out of Beckindale and Joe Sugden formed a new partnership with Alan Turner to buy Home Farm in January 1988. Meanwhile, Sandie bought The Mill herself.

New Blood Arrives

Sandie was joined in August 1988 by divorcée Kate Hughes and her teenage children, Rachel and Mark. Kate fell for Joe Sugden, in spite of the fact that on their first meeting he had shot her dog, Rex, for worrying sheep.

Mark found it hard to accept the relationship and, in January 1989, ran away with the intention of visiting his father in Germany. He failed to get further than Hull and, in February 1989, Kate left The Mill with her children to move in with Joe before marrying him.

Three months later, Sandie left for Scotland to be closer to her father, Tom, and illegitimate child, Louise, who had been adopted after her birth there six years earlier.

Dolly's Ordeals

Dolly Skilbeck moved into The Mill with son Sam in May 1989 following the breakdown of her marriage to farm labourer Matt, who finally left the village six months later after accepting that he and Dolly would never be reunited. In between, Dolly faced the ordeal of being kidnapped by local farmer Ted Sharp, who misread her friendship as something more, but she survived the ordeal.

To keep herself and Sam, Dolly took a job as housekeeper to Frank and Kim Tate at Home Farm in January 1990. Loyalty led Dolly to cover up for Frank's drinking bouts, and Frank's advances to her made Joe Sugden mistakenly think that she was having an affair with the new lord of the manor. After less than five months in her new job, Dolly decided to move out of her cottage and live in at Home Farm, although she subsequently bought 3 Demdyke Row from Joe Sugden as an investment.

Unexpected Delivery

One of the most dramatic events to take place at The Mill was the birth of Alice, daughter of Nick Bates and Elsa Feldmann, in February 1991. Elsa, on the way to a Valentine's Day register office marriage ceremony, went into premature labour and, in the absence of a midwife, had her baby delivered there by vet Zoë Tate.

Chris and Kathy Tate have The Mill bought as a wedding present for them by the groom's father, millionaire landowner Frank Tate.

A Wedding Present

Newlyweds Chris and Kathy Tate moved into The Mill in November 1991, when Chris's father, Frank, bought it as a wedding present for the couple. Chris's early, disastrous attempts at DIY annoyed Kathy, whose first husband, Jackie, had died in a shooting tragedy, but they were nothing compared with the selfishness and irresponsibility that he soon displayed in the marriage. Kathy tried to change her husband's 'Hooray Henry' manner, with little success.

The boorish Chris's old schoolfriend, Alex, became a house-guest with an open-ended invitation, which Kathy found trying. The two men also went out socially while Kathy was left at home, and Chris's attempts to placate her with flowers, wine and a bad-taste dress failed.

When Chris had a new fireplace installed at the cottage, Kathy was appalled by the smell that came from it. Eventually, she found out that he had bought it from Eric Pollard, who obtained it from the vicarage at neighbouring Robblesfield, which was next door to a slaughterhouse.

Chris lost his motorcycle to Alan Turner in a poker game, although Kathy was understanding when it emerged that he had done this as a result of his father usurping his power by taking part once more in the day-to-day operations of Tate Haulage, of which Chris was managing director. Kathy confronted Frank, asking him to leave the running of the company to Chris, and Frank persuaded Turner to hand back the bike – which he did, at a cost of £4000 – but Chris resented this interference.

Pastures New

Kathy left her labouring job at Emmerdale Farm to work at Kim Tate's Home Farm stables, but she quit in 1993 after discovering that Kim was cheating on husband Frank by having an affair with the Rt Hon. Neil Kincaid, not wanting to be a party to the deception. She became Chris's secretary at Tate Haulage but was determined to prove she was not just a dogsbody.

Following a number of disappearances, when Chris began to wonder whether she was having an affair, a giant haulage truck appeared with Kathy at the wheel, having qualified for an HGV licence.

Annie Finds Refuge

In the same year, Annie Sugden moved into The Mill temporarily with Chris and Kathy, whose first husband, Jackie, was the 'secret' son of Annie's son Jack. The matriarch of Emmerdale Farm did so after returning to Beckindale to find that Jack and brother Joe had moved everything out of the old farmhouse – declared unsafe because of subsidence – into Hawthorn Cottage and decorated a room for her without consultation.

She refused to attend the leaving party at the farmhouse or to join Jack and his girlfriend, Sarah Connolly, at Hawthorn Cottage and found temporary refuge with Kathy and Chris. But Annie's old friend Amos Brearly saved the day by suggesting that Hawthorn Cottage be renamed Emmerdale and she felt secure in moving into the Sugden family's new abode, even though she shortly afterwards bought herself a cottage in the village.

Son of his Father?

At the same time, Chris saw the opportunity to increase his power in the family business. His father was largely unaware of what was happening after hitting the bottle as a result of splitting up with wife Kim, so Chris tried to gain control of the Tate empire by buying Kim's shares – and, without Kathy's knowledge, taking out a mortgage on The Mill to get the £250,000 that enabled him to do so.

However, he was foiled when Frank secured daughter Zoë's backing so that Chris could not out-vote him on any decision and he ended up walking out on the business. His benevolent father gave him the chance to manage his Holiday Village, opened the previous year, but this proved unsuccessful and Chris – the boy born with a silver spoon in his mouth – was given yet another opportunity to make a success of himself by borrowing enough money from Frank to start his own haulage company, with just one truck.

Kathy's Doomed Affair

As Chris became embroiled in the quest for power, Kathy began to feel that she no longer knew the man she had married. On discovering that he had mortgaged their house, she withdrew all conjugal rights. The marriage was on a downward spiral and needed only the intervention of an outside party to end it.

That came with the arrival in Beckindale of suave American wine salesman Josh Lewis, who started visiting The Woolpack's wine bar, where Kathy was by now working – against Chris's wishes because it was managed by his sworn enemy, Lynn Whiteley, whom he regarded as a bad influence on his wife and blamed for encouraging his father to drink when stepmother Kim left him. Not surprisingly, Lynn was intent on helping to destroy Chris's marriage.

Eventually, Josh asked Kathy to leave Beckindale with him. She agreed but insisted that she would spend Christmas with the Tates first. The pair set a date of 30 December 1993 to go and, on that day, Kathy left a goodbye letter in The Mill. But the events of that evening turned Kathy and Josh's plans upside down.

The plane crash over Beckindale left Chris paralysed after being rescued from the Woolpack wine bar, which was hit by a fireball. As he was being dug out of the rubble, Josh – ever the gentleman – broke into The Mill to recover Kathy's letter, knowing that her guilt would not allow her to leave.

Mutual Confinement

As she faced the future with Chris, who was crippled for life and confined to a wheelchair, Kathy could muster no sympathy for him and soon regretted her decision to stay with him. Chris himself simply resented his lot and those who tried to help him.

A pep talk from sister Zoë persuaded him that he must face the future and she made him feel worthwhile by offering him work running the business side of her veterinary practice. But Chris still resisted all of his father's attempts to help, including the offer of a bungalow that would allow him to lead as normal a life as possible in his circumstances.

Seth Armstrong took temporary lodgings at The Mill in 1994 after losing his Demdyke Row cottage in the plane crash. Kathy's brother, Nick Bates, who lived in the same terrace, did the same – with daughter Alice – after leaving hospital, where he was treated for the trauma he had experienced in seeing his friend Archie Brooks killed by a fireball. He then accepted Frank Tate's offer to move into the nursery flat at Home Farm.

Kathy boils over as she returns to The Mill to find Chris proposing to Rachel Hughes, who is pregnant with his baby.

Rachel Lends Support

As Kathy – who began work at Frank Tate's new heritage farm – failed to give Chris the support he needed, he turned to young Rachel Hughes for comfort. They were thrown together first at Dr McAllister's surgery, where Rachel was receptionist. She managed to get Chris out of his wheelchair and into the swimming pool while Kathy looked on, apparently not concerned if his new friendship turned to romance.

The affair came out into the open on Guy Fawkes' Night 1994, the couple's third wedding anniversary, when Kathy saw Chris kissing Rachel. Despite her previous indifference, Kathy reacted fierily when, the following month, she found out that Rachel was pregnant.

Returning to The Mill, from which she refused to budge until a settlement was reached, and finding Chris and Rachel embracing one another, Kathy jumped on Rachel, grabbed her hair and wrestled the 'scarlet woman' to the ground. When Chris screamed that Rachel was pregnant, Kathy turned on her husband and pulled him out of his wheelchair.

Confused Kathy

A distressed Kathy then turned to village GP Bernard McAllister, on whom she developed a fixation. But he made it clear that he would not cheat on his wife, Angharad, and this was one of the events that led to the McAllister family leaving the village.

Confused, Kathy went to visit her mother in Scarborough and, in March 1995, Chris persuaded Rachel to move in with him. But Kathy returned to The Mill just as Chris was proposing to Rachel, and Kathy moved back in, insisting that she would stay until a fair divorce settlement was agreed. Eventually, after beginning a romance with Frank Tate's assistant farm manager Dave Glover, Kathy accepted £120,000 and bought the village's old school building to convert into tearooms.

Rachel's Unlikely Friend

Chris settled down to a life with Rachel, who had moved out of The Mill after Kathy's return, and

they accepted his father's invitation to live at Home Farm, moving in just before their son's birth on 8 June 1995.

The birth – six weeks early – was speeded up by the tragic news that Rachel's stepfather, Joe Sugden, had died in a car crash in Spain. Chris could not be contacted, so a terrified Rachel begged Kathy to stay with her. She did so and witnessed the birth of Joseph Mark, named as a tribute to both Rachel's stepfather and her brother Mark, who had died as a result of the 1993 air disaster.

This resulted in an unlikely friendship developing between Kathy and Rachel, which they kept secret from Chris. So it was a shock to him when Rachel insisted that Kathy be Joseph's godmother when he was christened.

Rachel's traumatic childbirth meant that she was unable to attend her stepfather's funeral when his body was brought back from Spain by his mother, Annie. Joe did not leave a will, so his share of Emmerdale Farm went to Annie, but she passed it on to Rachel's son to inherit on his eighteenth birthday.

Interfering Grandfather

At Home Farm, Rachel and Chris found that Frank was continually interfering in the baby's upbringing, so they moved back to The Mill after just a month. Chris was determined not to let Frank rule his life and the couple married in a quiet register office ceremony, with just Joseph and witnesses Jack and Sarah Sugden present, on 7 December 1995.

But Chris's worst traits returned as he plotted to gain revenge on his stepmother, Kim Tate, who had stripped him of power at Home Farm. Rachel walked out on Chris, and although she gave her marriage another chance it was clearly on the skids. He hoped for another child, but she continued to take the Pill.

Rachel's New Image

The arrival in Emmerdale of Rachel's former university friend Steve Marchant set in motion the events that were to lead to her split with Chris.

Steve, with his eye on Rachel, soon dispensed with girlfriend Faye Clarke. He asked Rachel to help him run his business, an independent financial consultancy, and made her feel good by taking her on shopping sprees to buy new clothes and enliven her image.

This fired Rachel's enthusiasm to be an independent woman with her own identity. But Chris was outraged when she joined campaigners demonstrating against Frank Tate's plans for a quarry in the village and she left him in October 1996. He moved back to Home Farm and, a month later, Rachel returned to The Mill with Joseph.

After ditching Tina Dingle, Steve romanced Rachel, who was furious when she discovered that he knew about Chris's £400,000 debts but had not told her, because it would affect her divorce settlement. Rachel finally dropped Steve after a row following a mistake she made that had cost his business thousands of pounds.

Frank Tate came to the aid of his son again when he offered Rachel The Mill as a divorce settlement and paid Chris the money for it.

A Shoulder for Jack

Looking for work, Rachel did a stint in the tearooms and helped out at Emmerdale Farm. When Jack offered her a full-time job, she accepted it and, as he and wife Sarah found themselves at odds over foster son Andy Hopwood's decision to return to his father, he used Rachel as a shoulder to cry on.

They started having an affair but, when Jack was found out, he did not take the opportunity to start afresh with Rachel. Instead, he felt guilty and tried for a reconciliation. Sarah eventually allowed him home, but only as a means of fostering Andy after his father turned to crime once more. The wounds inflicted on Jack and Sarah's marriage were far from healed. Meanwhile, Rachel found new employment as secretary at Hotten Comprehensive.

The Moving Mill

Over the years, The Mill has moved around the countryside in the *Emmerdale* storyline. It began as a derelict mill on Emmerdale Farm land, just across the river from the farmhouse and Hawthorn Cottage, at which time Jack Sugden moved in with the aim of converting it into living accommodation.

That never happened, and by the time his brother Joe and Phil Pearce began the conversion work in the 1980s, it had moved to the neighbouring village of Connelton and was called Colebrook Mill.

When it featured in the storyline again, the mill returned to the outskirts of Beckindale and – by the time Chris and Rachel Tate moved in – became known as Mill Cottage. While planning the building of the Harewood outdoor set, designer Mike Long moved it closer to the village and called it The Mill, a name befitting to its elegance and history.

On her own with son Joseph, Rachel falls for the charms of a more mature man – Jack Sugden.

Farrers Barn

Barn

1998–   Eric Pollard (antiques business downstairs),
Mandy Dingle (secondhand clothes shop upstairs)

CREATING REALITY

A new village property built when *Emmerdale* moved its outdoor filming to Harewood in 1998 was Farrers Barn.

'It was designed as a barn conversion for the Cairns family,' reveals designer Mike Long. 'It is divided into two, with a converted cottage on one side with living accommodation and a double-height barn on the other, intended to provide Becky with room for a pottery workshop and Tony with space at the upper level for his outward-bound equipment – as well as a good view to the pub and up the main street.

'The living area was intended to have oak beams, but I held fire on that and the workshop conversion when I heard that the Cairns were leaving the programme.'

In the event, the double-height barn was allocated to Eric Pollard at ground level for his antiques business and Mandy Dingle at the higher level for her new secondhand clothes enterprise.

A fter losing his licence at the wine bar, following a police raid that proved he was serving under-age drinkers, Eric Pollard sold the business to Kathy Glover and started relying on his previous experience as an antiques dealer to make a living.

Although he had continued to buy and sell items in often shady deals, it was almost ten years since he had ruled the roost at Hotten Market, where he gained a reputation as a dodgy dealer.

In 1998, Pollard started using the lower part of Farrers Barn for his business while Mandy Dingle took the upper level of the double-height barn to use for a secondhand clothes business.

Home Farm

1973	George and Laura Verney, Mark Proctor
1978	Gerald and Charlotte Verney
1978–9	Trevor and Paula Thatcher
1979–80	Maurice Westrop, Judy Westrop
1980–1	Richard Anstey
1981–2	Joe Sugden
1982–9	Alan Turner
1989–	Frank (1989–97) and Kim Tate (1989–98), Chris Tate (1989–91, 1995, 1996–), Zoë Tate (1989–91, 1992–5), Dolly Skilbeck (1990–1), Sam Skilbeck (1990–1), Rachel Hughes (1995), Joseph Hughes (1995), Dave Glover (1996), Sophie Wright (1996–7)

Nursery Flat

1990–1	Chris Tate and Kathy Merrick
1992–3	Joe Sugden, Mark Hughes (1993)
1994–5	Nick Bates, Alice Bates
1996	Kim Tate
1998	Kelly Windsor

CREATING REALITY

Creskeld Hall, a couple of miles from the new *Emmerdale* outdoor set, is the only location to survive the serial's entire run, although George Verney's manor house on the Miffield estate – known as the Hall – was not actually seen on screen until January 1973, once the programme had completed its initial, 13-week, 26-episode run and was guaranteed another 13 weeks on the ITV network.

The house's owner, who prefers to remain anonymous so that tourists do not descend on his property, still has a payment slip showing that his father received £25 from Yorkshire Television for the first day's filming at Creskeld Hall, which took place on 1 November 1972.

It had previously been used by the television company for filming scenes in programmes such as *Hadleigh*. In more recent years, Yorkshire has returned to use it as

a location in *The Sandbaggers*, *The Racing Game*, *The Darling Buds of May* and *Heartbeat*, as well as filming chef Anton Mosimann in the old kitchen using a coal-fired range for one of his popular series.

Although most Home Farm interiors are shot at the Emmerdale Production Centre, Creskeld Hall's estate office is used for indoor scenes, just as the bedroom and sitting room in the flat – occupied over the years by Joe Sugden, Nick Bates and others – have been.

Some of the owner's 300 acres of land – used for dairy farming – is a location for filming outdoor scenes set on the Home Farm estate. Shooting also took place for a while at Creskeld when a new location and cows were needed for Emmerdale Farm outdoor filming, following the retirement of

the farmer who lived at the farmhouse used for the Sugdens' home.

These days, the Home Farm scenes are usually done there one day in every fortnight, when those for six episodes are all shot together. However, schedules and scripts sometimes cause this to increase to as many as three days a week.

The only house rules are no smoking, no plastic cups, and cover everything up with dustsheets if the weather is wet and mess could be trodden into the building.

When the Emmerdale Production Centre moved to Leeds from Farsley, designer Mike Long took the opportunity to revamp the geography of the interior of Home Farm, which was also the serial's oldest set. 'I completely turned round the Home Farm composite set,' he says. 'At Farsley, it was designed to suit the studio layout and it was a nightmare.

'When we moved, I wanted all the backcloths to be on the same side, which they weren't in Farsley. The dining-room backcloth was on one side and the living-room one on the other, which takes up a huge volume of studio space.

'By doing that, I could also move all the doorways, which were opposite one another, so that you can look from the kitchen to the dining room, to the hall, through to the sitting room, and directors can use that dramatically.

'Apart from that, the biggest change I made was to the sitting room. The kitchen and the dining room, which is sometimes used as a meeting room, didn't really change. In the hallway, the front door matches Creskeld Hall.'

Only the Verney family, who had owned the Miffield estate in Beckindale since 1588, could boast a longer ancestry in the Beckindale area than the farming Sugdens. They lived in the manor house, a Grade II listed building known as the Hall, partly dating from the 17th century, on the 650-acre estate on the edge of the village, with 65 acres of mixed arable and rough grazing land, a 250-acre shoot, a fish farm and some smallholdings.

Tenant farmers leased land from the Verneys, who also owned a shop and various cottages around the village, and Sam Pearson – father of Annie Sugden – worked as a labourer for the estate and rose to become farm manager before his retirement. In fact, the estate was the biggest employer in Beckindale.

This feudal system continued into the 1970s, with the paternalistic lord of the manor George Verney still contributing a barrel of ale on village feast days. However, George's tenure proved to be the end of the line for the family.

George Verney is the last paternalistic lord of the manor in Beckindale.

Crumbling Empire

Signs of change began to show when, in 1972, Verney agreed to sell the freehold of Emmerdale Farm to incoming businessman Henry Wilks, who ensured that the land stayed in the Sugden family.

Then, the following year, Verney's wife, Laura – much younger than the squire himself – had an affair with Jack Sugden. When Jack also tipped off the *Hotten Courier* newspaper that a property company in which Verney had a majority shareholding was threatening to evict blacksmith Frank Blakey from his forge, the lord of the manor administered a public horsewhipping to the troublesome Sugden in front of The Woolpack. In the event, Jack accepted Verney's insistence that he knew nothing about the eviction plan.

NY Estates Steps In

Laura walked out on her husband shortly afterwards, the couple divorced and Verney spent the rest of his life in Cannes, leaving the manor house to be used as a teacher-training college in his absence. When he died in 1978, Gerald Verney, the squire's nephew and only heir following the death of his brother, arrived in Beckindale with his wife, Charlotte, to survey their inheritance.

Gerald was just a small-time London businessman who ran a company called Precosolv. He could not envisage a future with his inheritance after paying crippling death duties of £600,000,

Henry Wilks shows his daughter Marian's friend Francesca Zorelli a painting that is being sold after George Verney's death as the squire's nephew, Gerald, and his wife, Charlotte, sell the estate to pay death duties.

much to the disappointment of Charlotte, who longed to exchange the hustle and bustle of London for country life.

When Gerald put the house and estate up for sale, this caused great anxiety in the village because it had implications for the estate's workers and the properties that it owned. For traditionalists such as Sam Pearson, it meant the end of an era when the benevolent squire looked after the villagers, guaranteed their livelihood and could be relied on to attend local events. To Sam, the estate belonged to the village and he had no desire to see it pass into private ownership.

An advertisement in the *Hotten Courier* – 'The Hall, Miffield Rise, nr Beckindale … 10 bedrooms … built 1681' – was the first that villagers knew of the sale. As Gerald Verney looked at details of the estate, he discovered that the Sugdens were farming a 20-acre meadow, known as 'Top Twenty', that was not part of the freehold previously sold to Emmerdale Farm. It had simply been rented by Annie's late husband, Jacob, for a bottle of whisky a year – a payment known as the 'Verney Bottle'. A dispute with the Sugden family ended with them agreeing to pay for the land.

Humberside-based property conglomerate NY Estates stepped in to buy the rest of the Verneys' land and the Hall was renamed Home Farm. Trevor Thatcher, appointed the company's first manager in the village, arrived there with his wife, Paula.

During the sale of the Hall, a painting by Oswald Verney called *Dillingham Crags* was bought by Marian Wilks's Italian friend, Francesca Zorelli, for £230. It was later revealed that this work concealed a Caravaggio masterpiece, *The Flight of the Martyrs from the Lions* – worth about £200,000 – which had been covered up by moralist Oswald because the picture portrayed naked men and women.

Harsh Realities

One of Thatcher's first acts was to arrest Sam Pearson for poaching after missing the real culprit, Seth Armstrong. Fortunately, the matter was eventually dropped. Thatcher also erected signs warning the public not to trespass in the woods and gave 70-year-old Nellie Ratcliffe four weeks' notice to quit her cottage, where she had lived for the previous 48 years, so that he could give Steve Ashcroft a tied house when he took over as head cowman. Given the cold shoulder by villagers, Steve told Thatcher that he would not be taking up the job and Nellie was left in peace.

A Diplomatic Approach

Thatcher's time in Beckindale was short and unremarkable. In 1979, Maurice Westrop arrived to take over as estate manager and used diplomacy to engage Seth Armstrong, the wiliest poacher in Beckindale, as gamekeeper. He figured that this would significantly reduce poaching on NY Estates land, if only because Seth would not be doing any!

A greater challenge presented itself to Westrop when his daughter, Judy, arrived in Beckindale suffering from acute depression. She had turned to drink after having an abortion and was looking for family support. Westrop himself proved to be another short-lived NY Estates boss when the company transferred him to North Wales in 1980.

Ambitious Anstey

Richard Anstey, who had filled in during Westrop's absences, took over as estate manager and had firm ideas about how it should be run. With his ambition and dynamism, Anstey soon clashed with a shepherd and rowed with Henry Wilks over the development of forestry.

It seemed like a defection to the other side when, shortly after Anstey's arrival, Joe Sugden became his assistant manager at Home Farm, having become frustrated at Emmerdale Farm. Joe was becoming interested in new agricultural developments and saw this job as a new challenge.

Pawns in the Game

Anstey's personal life intrigued villagers, who were mystified by his wife Jenny's decision to spend most of her time in London. In 1981, Anstey showed bad judgement by launching into an affair with Virginia Lattimore, wife of NY Estates' much hated regional manager, Derek.

The arrival of Alan Turner as new estate manager in 1982 proves to be widely unpopular, especially with Joe Sugden, who is passed over for the job.

Home Farm. Until his successor could be appointed, Joe was made acting estate manager.

Turner Arrives

Joe had his own ideas about how the estate should be run and was, not surprisingly, disappointed to be passed over when NY Estates made its decision on appointing a new manager at Home Farm. So, when the inexperienced Alan Turner arrived to take up the post in March 1982, there was friction between the two men.

Alan's bull-in-a-china-shop approach was soon evident. He sought to rid himself of his jealous assistant by luring Matt Skilbeck from Emmerdale Farm, even offering the labourer Enoch Tolly's old farmhouse as an incentive – but in vain. Joe and the villagers also became used to Alan's lazy ways.

But the NY boss in Beckindale had no hesitation in sacking assistant gamekeeper Jackie Merrick, holding him responsible after a shooting party, held to impress the company's wealthy contacts, went wrong. Jackie's response was to set fire to the NY Estates caravan in which he lived, but he paid for this deed with a conviction for arson and 120 hours of community service.

Joe Moves On

It was Joe who had to take the blame when, two months after Alan's arrival, crop spraying from an NY helicopter resulted in some of brother Jack's herd of prize cattle stampeding. One heifer was killed and two others aborted. This resulted in a bitter argument, which was settled when NY Estates accepted that the pilot had been careless and paid compensation to Emmerdale Farm.

Joe found himself being used as a pawn in the game when Anstey opposed his idea of creating a new pig unit at Home Farm. Lattimore had doubts about its viability and sought to discredit Anstey by backing Joe and seeing the enterprise fail. Lattimore subsequently offered his wife a divorce, but it became apparent that Anstey had no intention of marrying Virginia. His sole aim had been to humiliate his boss.

It took the intervention of NY Estates managing director Christopher Meadows to resolve the problem. He insisted that Joe's proposal be tried out, with Lattimore supervising the project. When Anstey refused, he was sacked and thrown out of

Joe decided to leave Home Farm in October 1982 following the break-up of his romance with married woman Barbara Peters in the face of strong opposition from his family and Barbara's father, the Revd Donald Hinton. NY Estates found him a job in France, breeding Charollais on a beef ranch owned by the company, and he took the opportunity to escape his troubles.

Alan Takes Heed

Alan's drinking, womanising and gambling exploits eventually came to the attention of NY Estates' management. In 1984, managing director Christopher Meadows threatened to dismiss him unless he changed his ways.

Promising to turn over a new leaf, Alan attempted a reconciliation with his estranged wife, Jill. Although this did not work out, Jill was responsible during her brief stay at Home Farm for appointing Caroline Bates as Alan's secretary in an attempt to organise him and iron out his bad habits.

Caroline, who had recently split up from her womanising husband, Malcolm, moved to the village with her teenage children, Kathy and Nick. She was to prove a match for her boss and had no intention of letting Alan's bullishness and stubbornness force her out of the job.

Poachers Apprehended

An eventful year on the estate saw gamekeeper Seth Armstrong catch Tom Merrick, Derek Warner and Kevin Haynes poaching fish. Jackie Merrick, who believed Tom to be his father and was back in his job as assistant gamekeeper, blamed Seth for handing the gang over to the police. But Jackie took drastic measures himself when, after Emmerdale Farm sheep went missing, he shot Caroline Bates's dog on discovering it worrying the farm's flock.

Celebrations Turn Sour

Alan was in jubilant mood in 1985 when he beat Seth by a whisker to be elected a parish councillor. It was one of the early rounds fought by the boss and his employee in what was to become a battle of minds, with the wily gamekeeper seeking to outwit his pompous employer.

But the year also highlighted Alan's unhappy family history. He was finally divorced from wife Jill, and his lazy son, Terence, an Oxford University undergraduate, arrived at Home Farm after

being sent down. Alan made clear his disgust for Terence, who fell for Jackie Merrick's sister, Sandie.

Another unhappy event for Alan was a road accident in which his NY Estates Range Rover collided with Jackie, who was riding a new motorcycle. Fortunately, Jackie eventually recovered from his life-threatening injuries.

Joe Has Last Laugh

Further frustrations came for Alan when, in 1986, Joe Sugden returned from France and took his revenge for being passed over previously by taking the job of NY Estates regional manager – becoming Alan's immediate boss. However, Joe's decision to buy Hotten Market, so that NY could add the marketing side of farming to its activities, meant that he spent much time involved in that side of the business – and romancing market auctioneer Karen Moore.

Tough Times

On the Home Farm estate, Alan evicted Clifford Longthorn and his family – including son Andy, who fathered Sandie Merrick's love-child – from Lower Hall Farm when NY Estates needed the land. The Longthorns moved to Lincoln.

Seth Armstrong found himself vulnerable when he discovered a gang of badger-baiters trying to raid a sett. Beaten unconscious and left for dead, Seth was rushed to hospital, where he made a slow recovery from his head injuries and damaged ribs.

Uncertain Times

The Home Farm estate faced another major upheaval when, in 1987, NY Estates pulled out of Beckindale. Alan teamed up with Joe Sugden the following January to buy Home Farm and its land.

During 1988, Alan also received a year's driving ban after failing a breathalyser test. More serious crime reared its ugly head at Home Farm when Eric Pollard and Phil Pearce stole antique fireplaces. Pollard performed one of his many escape acts when police failed to find enough evidence to charge him with the robbery, but Phil confessed to the crime and was jailed.

The Tate family – Frank (left), second wife Kim, daughter Zoë and son Chris – take over Home Farm and look to a future that does not rely on the traditional industry of agriculture.

Alan's attempts at romance failed when a dating agency was unable to find him a suitable partner and, after spotting secretary Caroline Bates with Alan Walker, he made a play for Alan's partner, Rosemary, but that relationship came to nothing. However, his political ambitions were more successful and he beat newcomer Kate Sugden to win a seat on the district council.

Seeds of Change

Alan sold his Home Farm shares in October 1988 to crooked businessman Dennis Rigg, who wanted to establish a quarry in Beckindale and tried to acquire various properties in the village so that he could do so. Alan was instructed to get the Sugdens off their land, but this came to nothing as Rigg was crushed to death by a bull in July 1989 while wandering around the outbuildings at Emmerdale Farm.

Even after selling his shares, Alan continued as estate manager and, in the summer of 1989, Caroline encouraged him to start a fish and game farm on the estate. The pair, who finally found romance together, ran it in partnership. They planned to marry in December of that year, but the wedding was abandoned two months beforehand, when Caroline had to leave Beckindale to tend her sick mother in Scarborough.

Alan also lost his living accommodation at Home Farm when, in November 1989, it emerged that the estate had been sold for £1 million to Frank Tate, who set about putting into practice his plans to turn it into a modern-day, thriving business. However, Alan remained manager of the fish and game farm.

Frank's Vision

Self-made millionaire Frank, who had run a successful haulage business in Skipdale, arrived in Beckindale with second wife Kim, his former secretary whom he had married three years earlier following the death of his first wife, Jean.

Frank was taking early retirement at the age of 52 and handing over the reins of Tate Haulage to his son, Chris, who became managing director and moved into Home Farm, along with Frank's grown-up daughter, Zoë, who was training to be a vet. As well as allowing Frank to become lord of the manor in a retirement that was to prove extremely active, the move meant that Kim – who was almost half his age – was able to breed horses at Home Farm.

Calling a press conference to announce his plans, Frank made it clear that he intended to make the estate profitable by switching from the unviable business of farming to bringing tourism to the village, opening the fish farm to the public, expanding the game farm and creating both a museum of rural life and a championship-standard golf course.

Although not all of these aims were achieved, Frank had brought a new vision to a Dales village trapped in a reliance on agriculture, an industry that was in decline. However, he showed some signs of harking back to the days of the paternalistic Verneys by resurrecting the tradition of donating a cask of ale to the winners of the village's annual cricket match against Robblesfield.

A Frank Confession

At his first Hunt Ball, when the Demdale Hunt traditionally sets off from Home Farm each March, the first skeleton emerged from Frank's cupboard. George Starkey, a driver who had been sacked by Tate Haulage, arrived in a 32-ton 'artic' and claimed that Frank had killed his first wife so that he could marry Kim.

Frank, forthright as ever, made a public confession that he had, in fact, assisted Jean in killing herself in 1984 because she had been suffering from terminal cancer. He added that no charges had resulted from his 'mercy killing'.

Playing with Fire

Tackling the problem of making the estate profitable, Frank evicted widow Elizabeth Feldmann and her children, Michael and Elsa, from Keller Bottom Farm, at Blackthorn, in November 1990, after they fell £2000 behind with the rent.

When a Home Farm barn conversion was torched, Frank suspected Michael of being responsible for the arson attack in an attempt to gain revenge. But the culprit turned out to be NY Estates labourer Jock McDonald, who also organised illegal hare-coursing on Home Farm land. Jock was caught red-handed by Frank's daughter, Zoë, when she led a youth movement against local hare-coursers.

Pressures Mount

Zoë toyed with the idea of giving up her degree at Edinburgh University after the experience of meeting male chauvinists such as Joe Sugden and Alan Turner made her question her future. But her success in identifying the *Cryptodsporidium* outbreak at Emmerdale Farm, combined with a pep-talk from Jack Sugden, persuaded Zoë to return to her studies.

She graduated with honours in 1990, but Frank was not at the ceremony because he was suffering from the effects of a drinking session with old friend Terry Prince. He had hit the bottle after wife Kim expressed her desire to have a child of her own and he faced the prospect of a vasectomy reversal operation in the summer of 1990.

Keeping House – and Mum

Dolly Skilbeck, whom Frank had engaged as housekeeper at Home Farm in January 1990, became used to covering up for his drinking bouts. After four months in the job, she moved onto the premises with son Sam.

When Joe Sugden saw Frank making drunken advances to Dolly, who bought Joe's cottage in Demdyke Row, he thought the pair must be having an affair and using the house as a love-nest. In fact, she had simply bought it as an investment and later rented it out to Nick Bates.

Dolly had a relationship with crooked Hotten councillor Charlie Aindow, who arrived in Beckindale to claim back £2000 owed to him by Eric Pollard. When Dolly found out that he was married, Aindow insisted that he and his wife had

Home Farm housekeeper Dolly Skilbeck has an unhappy affair with crooked councillor Charlie Aindow before leaving Beckindale.

lived separate lives for years, although he was clearly worried when Eric Pollard threatened to phone his wife with news of his affair.

Eventually, Dolly sent Aindow packing after discovering that he and his wife were still together. Later finding herself pregnant, she decided on an abortion. Also humiliated at work after Frank tried to use her charms to secure a contract with groping wealthy industrialist Arthur Bright, Dolly left Beckindale in August 1991 to seek pastures new in Norfolk.

Love for Chris

Frank's son, Chris – who was born with a silver spoon in his mouth and had always lived in the shadow of his father – found love with Kathy Merrick, who was still grieving the tragic death of her first husband, Jackie, in a shooting accident. Chris moved into the nursery flat at Home Farm and was pleased when Kathy joined him there.

She tried to temper his selfishness – for example when Chris irritated his father by confronting him about having the operation to reverse his vasectomy. Kathy tried to make Chris realise that it was Frank's decision whether he wanted children with Kim and that he risked breaking up the family by interfering.

Chris showed a rare, touching side to his character when he wrote a song for Kathy called 'Just This Side of Love', which she sang at a village hall concert. Secretly recording the performance, he had it made into a record, which a surprised Kathy first heard on the Woolpack jukebox. Chris also sprayed one of the records gold, framed it and gave it to Kathy as a present.

Ups and Downs

Frank showed himself to be community-minded by arranging a free game shoot for villagers on New Year's Day 1991, with a free bottle of champagne as the prize. Elizabeth Feldmann might have felt it no compensation for the loss of her farm when she was proclaimed best shot, but she was able to face a brighter future when Alan Turner appointed her secretary, then manager, at the fish and game farm,

with its office in the tied cottage at 17 Main Street (now Victoria Cottage).

But Tate Haulage was hit badly in 1991 when it lost its biggest customer, and Frank put the yard lease up for sale. With business problems getting worse and no money put aside to pay VAT, Frank considered hijacking one of his own lorries to claim the insurance. But Kim bailed him out by selling a horse for £35,000. Frank had already upset Chris by taking a greater interest in the daily running of Tate Haulage in his position as chairman.

Children and Animals

Zoë, who took a job at Martin Bennett's veterinary practice in Hotten in August 1990 after qualifying, found herself dealing with people, not animals, when she delivered Elsa Feldmann and Nick Bates's baby daughter, Alice, at The Mill the following February. This emergency action came when the teenage mother-to-be went into labour on the way to her planned register-office wedding ceremony.

Later, joining a local animal rights movement through her friendship with activist Archie Brooks, Zoë discovered that her employer's practice was the target of a demonstration. Realising that Bennett was involved in animal experiments, she left her job there and looked for a new challenge by becoming a flying vet in New Zealand.

Wedding Bells

Chris finally made it to the altar with Kathy Merrick after an on-off romance. At one point, Kathy was showered with attention from the Revd Tony Charlton, Beckindale's new curate, whose quiet charms were a marked contrast to Chris's brashness and arrogance. But Tony, who was infatuated with Kathy, left for London after realising that she still loved Chris.

The wedding took place at Hotten Register Office on 5 November 1991, after Chris and Kathy refused Frank's offers of a lavish ceremony. But Frank ensured that the rest of their day met his high expectations, having them flown by helicopter from Hotten to Home Farm for an expensive reception, followed by a spectacular firework display

that concluded with a giant burning heart containing the names of Kathy and Chris.

To complete his show of generosity, Frank also bought The Mill as a wedding present for the couple, although both continued to visit Home Farm on a daily basis through their work there.

Frank's Holiday Village Opens

The big event of 1992 on the Home Farm estate was Frank realising his ambition of opening a holiday village in the summer, with manager Joe Sugden taking accommodation in the nursery flat. Once again, he was looking for a fresh start, this time after the break-up of his marriage to Kate, following her prison sentence for killing Pete Whiteley in a road accident.

When the *Hotten Courier* found out about Chris taking part in the horse-meat trade by shipping old animals to the Continent for domestic consumption, Frank prevented bad publicity in the newspaper by threatening to withdraw advertising for the Holiday Village. Frank also took over the fish farm on the estate, but left Alan Turner – who had

Frank Tate's wealth is on show as he has son Chris Tate and bride Kathy Merrick flown from their register-office wedding to Home Farm for a lavish reception.

become landlord of The Woolpack the previous year – to run the game reserve.

Robbery and Battery

Frank turned down Michael Feldmann's request to let him take over George Winslow's tenant farm when the old man died in 1992, instead earmarking it for the opening of a model farm for those at the Holiday Village. So, less than two years after his family had been evicted from their farm on the estate, Michael sought revenge.

He joined the Rt Hon. Neil Kincaid's stable-hand, Steve Marshal – who was helping out on the estate – in a robbery at Home Farm. While Steve and his accomplices stripped the house of all the valuables they could lay their hands on, Michael looked on, bewildered.

When the gang started destroying the artefacts they could not carry away, Joe Sugden heard the

Frank gives his wife's lover, the Rt Hon. Neil Kincaid, a horse-whipping at the 1993 New Year's Day hunt.

noise, came to investigate and was clubbed by one of them. Michael stood dumbfounded as Steve and the others set off, leaving Joe lying unconscious on the floor. He carefully placed a cushion under Joe's head before joining the exodus.

Then, dodgy dealer Eric Pollard arranged a meeting with the gang – minus Michael – when they tried to offload the goods. But Pollard tipped off the police, who arrested Steve and his accomplices. Officers caught up with Michael later, as he left church following his mother Elizabeth's wedding to Pollard, and he ended up being jailed for four months.

Kim Falls for Kincaid

Kim was confined to a wheelchair after breaking her leg through falling off her horse at the Hotten Show in 1992. But the fall had more far-reaching consequences when Kim admitted to Frank that she had secretly been pregnant and had lost the baby.

She subsequently decided against having children, which disappointed Frank, who had set his heart on another child after having his vasectomy-reversal operation.

The new Master of the Foxhounds, the Rt Hon. Neil Kincaid, an aristocratic landowner in the district, volunteered to help Kathy Tate at the Home Farm stables while Kim was out of action. He also helped Frank to set up his model farm. However, it was Kim on whom Kincaid had set his sights and, when horse-dealing activities took them on visits away, the pair started an affair.

When Kathy found out about Kim's infidelity, she left her job at the stables, not willing to cover up for Kim. She became Chris's secretary at Tate Haulage and even qualified for her HGV licence in an attempt to prove that she was not just a dogsbody.

Kim's affair came out into the open at Christmas, when Frank looked forward to a family reunion following the return of Zoë from New Zealand. He also waited with enthusiasm for the elegant wristwatch he had seen among Kim's Christmas shopping. Having once again conquered his over-reliance on drink, Frank happily sipped orange juice while everyone else quaffed champagne.

But his feeling of well-being was transformed after he saw Kincaid wearing the watch on his visit to the house and he received a pair of rare sporting prints from his wife. Boiling over with anger, Frank threw Kim out of the house then and there in her skimpy cocktail dress. Kim moved in with Kincaid and Frank turned back to his old friend, the bottle.

Frank's Revenge

Frank exacted revenge first by dragging Kincaid from his horse and horse-whipping him at the New Year's Hunt. Determined to remove all traces of Kim from his life, Frank then shredded her dresses and planned to sell her horses.

When he refused to hand over her cherished filly Dark Star, Kim and Kincaid mounted a night-time raid on the stables. They were met by Frank with a shotgun. Daughter Zoë's swift action in knocking the weapon up in the air prevented him from shooting the horse and Kathy later returned Dark Star to Kim.

However, Kim – who reverted to her maiden name of Barker – began to find the experience of life with her aristocratic lover different from what she had expected. He tried to mould the former secretary into the lady of the manor and was critical of her dress sense and taste in décor. Mixing in Kincaid's social circle also proved embarrassing when she revealed to his friends that her mother was a hairdresser.

The final straw came when Kincaid thought he was doing Kim a favour by setting her up in new stables. They were to run the business as a partnership, but he revealed that he had already arranged for architects and builders to change the premises according to his specifications. As a result, she walked out on him and the affair was over. Hearing of this, Frank hoped for a reconciliation. He arranged a meeting with Kim at a hotel and broached the subject, but his estranged wife made it clear that she had no intention of returning to him.

Frank then made life hell for his employees at Home Farm. When Seth refused to shoot herons who had been eating trout at the fish farm because it was illegal to shoot these protected birds, Frank grabbed a gun and was only prevented from doing so himself when assistant gamekeeper Mark Hughes intervened and Eric Pollard arrived to calm the situation.

Frank also threatened Joe Sugden with the sack if he continued to see Kim, who visited the Holiday Village to appraise its value in a divorce settlement. As a result, Joe resigned and became manager of Kim's stables, while Chris took over his job at the Holiday Village.

A Family Torn Apart

Set firmly on a downward spiral, Frank found consolation in the whisky bottle and was flattered by the attentions of young widow Lynn Whiteley, who had hopes of running a leisure centre at the Holiday Village and saw the chance to profit from the situation.

Encouraged by Lynn, Frank adopted a new image, appearing in The Woolpack in a bright pink jacket and black shirt open to the neck. After proposing to Lynn and being politely rejected, Frank invited her to dinner at Home Farm and ended the evening by suggesting that she stay the night, but Lynn again refused.

Frank's business was suffering, too. His bank manager refused money for expansion and Frank himself scuppered a business deal that Chris was on the verge of clinching when he reversed into the client's car. Kim threatened Frank with a minority shareholders' action to take away his control of the business on the grounds that he was unfit to run it and was heading towards bankruptcy.

A power battle followed in which Chris colluded with Kim to oust Frank. He took out a mortgage on The Mill – without telling wife Kathy – so that he could buy Kim's shares for £250,000. The money enabled Kim, who was living in a caravan, to buy new stables.

But Chris was foiled in his attempt at gaining control of the Tate empire when Frank secured daughter Zoë's backing so that he could not be outvoted on business decisions. Chris was stripped of his power at Tate Haulage and appointed manager of the Holiday Village. His spell there proved disastrous and he was given another chance when his father, anxious to make peace, loaned him the money to start his own haulage business with just one truck.

Frank finally pulled back from the brink and stopped drinking after an old flame, Ruth Jameson, visited the Holiday Village, although they did not resume the romance that had once almost led to the altar. Ruth left after realising that Frank still carried a torch for Kim.

Zoë's Lesbian Confession

The sensitivity that Frank displayed when Zoë confessed to him that she was a lesbian led to her agreement to back him on business decisions. Zoë's realisation about her sexuality came after she resumed her friendship with Archie Brooks and ended up in bed with him.

Reunited after the plane crash, Frank and Kim enjoy their second wedding, at Ripon Cathedral.

pull Kim away screaming as she tried to save Dark Star and her other beloved horses.

Frank then set about masterminding the rescue operation, supervising Jack Sugden in laying pipes with his tractor to act as a second bridge for rescue vehicles to enter the village after the first was blocked by a broken-down lorry.

While some villagers died in the tragedy, the Tates survived, though the injuries that Chris sustained left him paralysed after he was dug from the rubble of The Woolpack's wine bar. Getting their lives into perspective, Frank and Kim entered 1994 together again.

Brother and Sister

Nick Bates, the Home Farm gardener who was traumatised and temporarily blinded as a result of the plane crash, was grateful to Frank for being offered accommodation in the nursery flat following the destruction of his own cottage in Demdyke Row.

He also faced a custody battle with ex-girlfriend Elsa Feldmann over their daughter, Alice, whom he had brought up single-handedly since Elsa had left for Leeds and a life with no responsibilities. In her attempt to win back the girl, Elsa even claimed that Nick and Archie Brooks, his childminder who had died in the disaster, were gay and cited an incident in which Alice had hurt her head after pulling over an ironing board. However, a court decided in Nick's favour and he hoped for happier times ahead.

Nick's sister, Kathy Tate, started work at the new model farm after a stint at the Woolpack wine bar, which was demolished in the disaster. She had planned to elope with wine salesman Josh Lewis on the night of the tragedy, but felt a sense of duty to stay with Chris after seeing his injuries. However, she could not give her husband the support he needed and he eventually fell for Rachel Hughes.

She subsequently admitted to Archie that she had done this to test her feelings and now knew that she could not have a sexual relationship with any man.

Coming to terms with her sexuality, Zoë sought to meet others like her by visiting a gay group in Leeds but was unimpressed by the poetry reading she had to sit through.

United in Disaster

By Christmas 1993, Frank was set on reconciliation and determined to put the events of the previous year behind him. On 30 December, as he drove to Kim's stables with a belated seasonal gift that he hoped might heal the wounds, Frank witnessed the disaster of a plane crashing over Beckindale.

When he arrived at the stables, they were alight. With help from Vic Windsor, Frank sought to put out the fire, but it proved too much and he had to

A New Start

The heritage farm opening was marred by Frank

Home Farm is the scene of Zoë and Emma's first kiss.

suffering a heart attack while driving home at the end of the day, leaving him in hospital close to death. Kim subsequently took over management of the game farm and appointed Dave Glover as gamekeeper. His predecessor, Seth Armstrong, found a new job as heritage farm warden.

After recovering from his heart attack, Frank concentrated on the wedding plans. He had caught the bridal bouquet at Jack and Sarah Sugden's wedding and promptly proposed to Kim. The couple remarried at Ripon Cathedral on 22 December 1994, laid on a lavish wedding party for the villagers and set off for a dream honeymoon in Hawaii. They seemed to have reconciled their differences.

Zoë Moves Out

After setting up her own veterinary surgery at the heritage farm in 1994, Zoë came to terms with her own identity. It was at Home Farm the following year that she exchanged her first lesbian kiss, taking Emma Nightingale back after the designer had celebrated winning a contract to give The Woolpack a new look.

Emma stayed at Home Farm with Zoë while Frank and Kim honeymooned. Then the couple moved into the village's old forge, converting it into a cottage and veterinary surgery, with room for Emma to work, and renaming it Smithy Cottage.

Overbearing Grandfather

Chris's romance with Rachel Hughes, who moved into The Mill with him before his marriage to Kathy was officially over, led to Rachel becoming pregnant. Frank invited Chris and Rachel to move into Home Farm shortly before the premature birth of son Joseph in June 1995.

It soon became evident that Frank wanted to heap as much fuss and attention on his grandson as he could. He even announced that he had enrolled Joseph at a private school. As a result, Chris and Rachel moved back to The Mill the following month and married in a quiet register-office ceremony at the end of the year.

KIM'S TRAGIC AFFAIR

Kim, who with Chris had been opposed to Frank's appointment of Dave Glover as assistant farm manager in 1995, went on to seduce the former gamekeeper in a romance that had echoes of *Lady Chatterley's Lover*.

When Frank sent Dave to a conference in a Leeds hotel, Kim arranged to meet him there. Dropping by to see how Dave was getting on, Frank narrowly missed catching his employee and wife together in bed. He even paid Dave a bonus in recognition of the extra work he was putting in, not realising that some of it was with Kim.

When Dave dumped Kim and became engaged to Kathy, the lady of the manor exacted revenge by sacking Kathy's brother, Nick Bates, from his job as gardener at Home Farm. As a result, he also lost his accommodation in the nursery flat. After finding out the reason for his dismissal, Nick tried to blackmail Kim, but she silenced him by trampling him with her horse. Although she subsequently reinstated Nick in his job, Kim made threats against his daughter Alice in the event of any similar incident.

Still ignorant of her affair, Frank was overjoyed when Kim announced that she was pregnant. But, when he heard Dave discussing with Biff whether he was the father, Frank turned to drink and was rushed into intensive care when his liver failed. He walked out of hospital to spy on Kim and Dave together again at Home Farm but was rushed back to intensive care, critically ill.

Chris then took on Kim in a battle for control of Tate Holdings. She was victorious in the battle – and Chris's obsession with plotting against his stepmother led to wife Rachel leaving him and Chris returning to live at Home Farm, although she did give their marriage another chance later.

Another relationship appeared to be over when Kathy called off her engagement to Dave after discovering that he was seeing Kim again. Frank, not letting Kim and Dave know that he was aware of the affair, plotted his own revenge. He offered Dave a cottage on the Home Farm estate and used Pete McCarty, a private investigator friend, to install cameras and microphones. These were connected to Frank's computer and, when he saw the pair in bed together, he walked in on them.

Dave was sacked but Kim refused to leave Home Farm, although she was persuaded to sign away her rights to Frank's fortune. Kim retaliated by moving Dave into Home Farm, but he was worn down by the constant bickering and, when Frank presented them with video evidence of their affair, it was the final straw for Dave and he moved into Tenant House.

Kim followed him there and Frank, told by her that the baby she was carrying was not his, started divorce proceedings. But he used his money and power to persuade Kim, in May 1996, to accept £1 million in return for leaving Dave, returning to Home Farm, putting his name on the baby's birth certificate and living with him for the first year of the baby's life. Kim did so but told Dave that she was going home because Frank was really the father of her baby.

Living in an attic room with bars on the window, and tended by a full-time nurse, Kim began to feel like a prisoner, so she moved into the nursery flat. She gave birth to a son, James Francis, on 24 September 1996 but showed little love for him, leaving him in hospital to return home to see her beloved horse, Valentine, when he was taken ill. Kim was devastated to find that Zoë had put him down.

Dave still believed himself to be the father of Kim's baby, but Frank would not let him near his wife. As a result, he returned to Kathy and married her in November 1996. Just a month later, as Kim began to warm to James, she told Dave that they could all start a new life together away from Emmerdale.

Dave was torn between Kim and new wife Kathy but, leaving his sister Linda's wedding reception, he met Kim at Home Farm, where she was ready to leave, bags packed. Frank then returned and had

a confrontation with the couple outside the house.

As they spotted a fire starting in the nursery, Dave raced up the stairs to rescue James from his cot. With flames engulfing the building, Dave was only able to hand the baby out through a narrow window. As he himself tried to escape, Dave was hit by a falling curtain pelmet and sustained severe burns.

Two days later, on Boxing Day 1996, he died from those injuries and lung damage. Kim discovered that she was indirectly responsible for Dave's death because the fire was caused by her beauty products exploding. Emmerdale's most tragic double love triangle was over.

But Kim left villagers bewildered when she attended Dave's funeral, throwing a rose onto the coffin before Kathy, his widow, had a chance to do so herself and telling her rival in love that Dave had planned to leave with her. However, Frank subsequently revealed that blood tests he had arranged proved that Dave could not be the father of James.

Left   Kim cheats on Frank again as she falls for his bright-eyed assistant farm manager Dave Glover.

Below   Dave saves Kim's baby son, James, in a blaze in the Home Farm nursery but dies himself of burns and lung damage.

Zoë discovers father Frank's dead body, unaware of her stepmother's part in his death.

Like Father, Like Son

Frank had hired Tina Dingle as his personal assist-ant at the height of the troubles at Home Farm. This annoyed both Kim and Chris. But Tina walked out on Frank after he tried to move the relationship onto a more personal level.

As Chris himself played dirtier and dirtier, Rachel left him for good and began divorce proceedings. After a bitter battle, in which her husband claimed bankruptcy and refused to agree a settlement, Frank forced Chris to let Rachel have The Mill.

Sinking to his lowest depths, Chris started black-mailing Linda Fowler into being 'nice' to him to ensure that husband Biff kept his job as estate manager. After unsuccessfully trying to rape Linda, Chris was kidnapped at gunpoint by her father, Ned, and was lucky not to be killed.

Prison and Plots

In the bitterness that continued into 1997, Kim sold her livery business and golf course shares to Chris for £350,000, but he was later to discover that she had swindled him out of these and there was no record of his ownership.

Then Frank accused Kim of tipping off the Inland Revenue about an alleged tax fraud by him

and Chris. This resulted in a row, during which Kim scratched Frank's face before disappearing, without baby James. A police search was eventually mounted. After her car was recovered from the bottom of a quarry, Frank identified the dead body inside as that of Kim.

He was then arrested for her murder, charged and held in prison on remand. Kim's will left her estate to Zoë, but Chris insisted that she was incompetent to run Home Farm in his father's absence. When Chris told his father that Zoë planned to sell, and tried to extract £700,000 from him to buy back the company and keep it in the family, Frank refused, saying that Chris had bought out Kim and was double-crossing him. He also instructed Zoë to appoint Steve Marchant as acting manager of Tate Holdings.

Caught in the crossfire at Home Farm, Sophie Wright – who had been James's nanny since his birth – found a friend in Zoë. When Chris's bitch-ing became too much, Zoë invited Sophie to move in at Smithy Cottage with her. She did so and a relationship followed as the nanny responded to the vet's advances.

Frank was released from prison when the Director of Public Prosecutions decided that the police had no case against him. He was bitter towards Chris because of his deal with Kim and sacked Steve, claiming that he was trying to con him. So, when Steve managed to buy 20 per cent of the company's shares behind Frank's back, he was furious.

Kim Returns from the Dead

Frank had the shock of his life when, on 22 May 1997, Kim reappeared at Home Farm as he sat alone watching television. Wearing gloves to avoid leaving fingerprints, Kim took Frank's heart pills from a kitchen drawer as she entered the house.

On seeing her, Frank broke down in Kim's arms and said he could not believe she was alive. But he then turned on his wife, wanting to know where she had been. Kim explained that she had hired another woman to drive her car before going to Mauritius, setting Frank up for her murder.

As she became menacing towards him, Kim claimed that Frank had killed the wrong woman and said she would go to the police and clear his name if he would let her take James away. He refused to do any deals, grabbed Kim and, in the struggle that followed, suffered a heart attack. As he pleaded with her to call an ambulance, Kim just stood still as he fell into an unconscious state, before leaving the house as quietly as she had arrived. The following morning, a distraught Zoë discovered Frank's dead body.

Building Her Empire

Everyone was speechless when Kim turned up at Frank's funeral. It was the first they had seen of Frank's wife since her supposed death. She immediately set about building her empire after inheriting Frank's estate. Feeling a debt to Jan Glover, whose son Dave had died saving her baby, Kim gave her a job as housekeeper at Home Farm – but put her in her place by insisting that she wear a uniform. She also paid for Jan's remaining son, Roy, to have driving lessons.

As Chris came to terms with Kim being in charge, he stayed but had to endure his stepmother's new alliance with Steve Marchant. She bedded the financial whiz-kid but had no qualms about trying to do the same with Lord Alex Oakwell after putting her own money into his ailing stud business, against Steve's advice. Alex continued to make a play for Kim even after he married Tara Cockburn.

Steve then proposed to Kim, adding that he would give her his share in Tate Holdings once they were married. She accepted and, at their engagement party, set up Linda Glover with a drugged-up Alex, who took her away in Steve's car, crashed and left Linda to die. The aristocrat immediately left the country and Kim took part in the cover-up.

James's 'Kidnap' Drama

Christmas 1997 proved to be another dramatic one for Kim as James went missing after her return from New Zealand, where she had visited a horse breeder. Kim was certain that James had been kidnapped for a ransom, but a deranged Jan Glover was arrested on being found with James at St Mary's Hospital, Hotten, talking to him as if he were her late son, Dave, when he was a little boy. A judge ensured that Jan received medical attention and Kim was relieved to get James back unharmed.

Blackmail Threat

Money was on one person's mind when Kim started receiving blackmail threats. Steve tackled the blackmailer, Jimmy Daniels, who claimed to have been hired by Kim to frame Frank for murder by getting a woman to drive her car, which ended up at the bottom of the quarry.

Steve paid Daniels £10,000 for a video that showed Kim's meeting with him. Although he told Kim that he had destroyed the video without viewing it, Steve played it and heard his fiancée tell Daniels that she did not care what happened to the woman as long as Frank ended up in jail.

Chris and Zoë were subsequently horror-struck to learn of this and, when he confronted Daniels, Chris was dumbfounded to hear that the fixer had not murdered the woman – his father, Frank, had. Then Zoë discovered a garage receipt showing that Frank had had repairs done to the bumper of his car at the time of the murder. Her illusions about her father had been shattered.

The current house at Creskeld Hall – mostly built in the past 150 years but with some parts dating back to the 17th century – is on the site of the original manor house, which was on low-lying land and protected by a moat, parts of which still exist. The Saxon hamlet of Creskeld, a few miles outside Leeds, is steeped in history.

In 1189, Hugh de Creskeld gave all his land there to Kirkstall Abbey, which added a chapel to the squire's residence. At the time of of the dissolution of the monasteries, in the 16th century, the manor passed into the hands of Thomas Cranmer, a nephew of Henry VIII's famous Archbishop of Canterbury.

Down the years, it passed through different families until the present owner's grandfather bought the estate in 1919. His son-in-law, an MP, agreed to let Yorkshire Television use it as the location for the manor house – later called Home Farm – in *Emmerdale*'s early days on screen. Since his death in 1973, shortly after filming began, the MP's son – who inherited Creskeld Hall on his mother's death 20 years later – has allowed filming to continue.

One point of interest outside the house itself is a gargoyle with water pouring out alongside a nearby stream. The gargoyle itself came from Bradford's Swan Arcade, which was demolished in the 1960s, and the stone crest underneath it was once part of the exterior of the House of Commons, rescued from the rubble when the Houses of Parliament were bombed during the Second World War.

Chris Conned

When Holiday Village chalet maid Kelly Windsor persuaded Chris to appoint her as his personal assistant, he started a game of flirtation that was to give her a route out of her dilemma when she became pregnant after a one-night stand with Biff Fowler in November 1997. Kelly succumbed to Chris's desires, then announced that she was expecting his baby.

Kelly expected her boss to pay for an abortion, but he saw this as perhaps his final chance to have another child and moved her into the nursery flat at Home Farm. However, Kelly's initial wish was granted in the most violent way during a party staged for some of Chris's business clients, when she went to Kim's room and put on one of her best dresses.

Kim appeared and argued with Kelly, who went tumbling down the stairs after Kim grabbed her. Although the teenager suffered only bruises, she miscarried and later regretted losing her baby. She then returned to her parents at the post office and would have nothing more to do with Chris.

Kim's Demise

During this time, Chris had gone into business with Lady Tara Oakwell to launch an activity centre in the village, which was the brainchild of retired Army major Tony Cairns. He looked on with satisfaction as Kim and Steve lost all their money and faced ruin.

Kim Tate finds a new husband in Steve Marchant but starts life penniless after his disastrous investment of her money and his own.

As Steve's business went downhill, Kim put all her own money into it. When it collapsed, at the time of their wedding on 7 May 1998, the couple had no choice but to sell their controlling interest in Home Farm.

As they adjusted to life without money in Steve's small cottage, and Steve accepted work as a labourer, Lady Tara Oakwell bought the couple's shares. When Tara's own father died, leaving her with huge death duties, asset-stripping and evictions on the Home Farm estate were at the front of her astute business mind.

Tara also saw a means of making money by marrying another aristocrat, Lord Michael Thornfield, and leaving her lawyer in charge at Home Farm, with Chris and Zoë retaining a minority shareholding in the empire that their father had built up. The question remained whether Kim and Steve, after hitting rock bottom, would fight their way back.

Shortly before taking control of Home Farm, Lady Tara Oakwell employs Biff Fowler as her chauffeur.

Home Farm's most dramatic storyline, the death of Dave Glover in 1996 after he tried to rescue his lover Kim Tate's baby son from the upstairs nursery, which was engulfed in flames, called for a change to the front of Creskeld Hall that viewers never even noticed – an extra floor built on top of the building so that none of the property suffered damage.

It was the biggest fire ever staged by Yorkshire Television. Interiors were filmed over 12 hours inside Studio 3 of its main building in Leeds instead of at the Emmerdale Production Centre. All exteriors and several interior shots were filmed at Creskeld Hall.

Production controller Tim Fee is used to filming there going smoothly, simply booking the days required and hearing nothing from its owner. However, the morning after set designer Barbara Shaw had another storey built on top of Creskeld Hall, he received a phone call from the owner.

'He never, ever phones me,' says Tim. 'I phone *him*. But the phone rang at 8.30am and I knew there was a problem. He's a terribly polite gentleman and he said, "I just thought I'd phone you to tell you about the nursery – it's in my front garden." It had been blown off the roof by gales.' As a result, filming was delayed for two weeks while the frontage was rebuilt.

Special effects designer Ian Rowley – responsible for the spectacular *Emmerdale* plane crash three years earlier – masterminded the fire scenes. Fire bars and fans were used to strike up huge gushes of flames inside the room.

A blazing curtain pelmet that fell on Dave in the story dropped within inches of a stuntman who jumped clear and scuttled across the floor in a meticulously planned stunt, as an enormous fireball was blown out of the window in one of the serial's most suspenseful scenes.

But Creskeld Hall's owner, who watched as it was filmed, is used to the tricks of television. 'The special effects are so well controlled,' he says, 'that the eventual fire was a bit of a damp squib. There was 20 seconds of fire, then they blew the window out. But it was filmed in the dark, so it was quite spectacular.'

Holiday Village

The opening of Home Farm's Holiday Village provides Frank Tate with one of the proudest days of his life.

CREATING REALITY

The holiday village site, containing cabins for holidaymakers, has been filmed at Rudding Park, three miles south of Harrogate, since Frank Tate started this venture on screen in 1992. In real life, the 50-acre holiday park opened 21 years earlier, shortly after the Mackaness family took over the 2000-acre estate.

The original house at Rudding Park was bought by Lord Loughborough in 1788 and he commissioned the renowned garden designer Repton to improve the surrounding landscape. Building of the present house, a Grade I listed building with Regency architecture, was started after the Hon.

William Gordon bought the estate in 1805 and completed after he sold it to Sir Joseph Radcliffe 19 years later.

Since the Mackaness family took over in 1972, they have implemented leisure developments such as the holiday park and a golf course. Rudding Park House was opened as a conference and banqueting centre in 1987 and, ten years later, a 50-bedroom hotel next to the house opened its doors to the public.

Rudding Holiday Park, with areas for touring caravans and campers, as well as mobile homes, lodges and cottages, has won many awards.

Frank Tate's greatest ambition when he bought the Home Farm estate in 1989 was to open a holiday village in an effort to bring tourism to Beckindale. Inevitably, there was some local opposition to filling part of the landscape with chalets for holidaymakers, and crooked Hotten councillor Charlie Aindow tried to get money from Frank in return for ensuring that the planning committee approved the development. But Frank refused to accept a bribe, and wife Kim sent Aindow off with a briefcase full of horse manure.

The scheme was accepted by the council and Frank took great pride in unveiling the Holiday Village in May 1992, with the Lady Mayoress of Hotten performing the official opening ceremony – despite Aindow trying to ruin the event by double-booking her.

But the day still did not run quite as smoothly as Frank had hoped. It started with a cocktail party in honour of the Mayoress that went over schedule when a gas leak was discovered on the village site.

Finally, the leak was tracked down to one of the chalets and the opening went ahead.

Joe Runs the Show

Joe Sugden had left Emmerdale Farm four months earlier when Frank head-hunted him as manager of the Holiday Village, crossing Beckindale as he had previously done when he joined NY Estates.

Although Frank was known as a demanding boss and Joe had reservations about working for him, he quickly made a favourable impression by producing the official Holiday Village brochure in just a few days. The pictures of 'summer' events were shot in January using models such as Seth Armstrong, Rachel Hughes, Jack Sugden and Lynn Whiteley posing in clothes totally unsuitable for the winter temperature.

After organising the brochure, Joe set off across Europe on a fact-finding trip to similar holiday sites. On his return, he was disconcerted to find Frank uninterested in his report and arranging with Lynn

Whiteley the contract for a shop. However, Chris and Kim confronted Frank with Joe's grievances and he agreed to hand over the reins completely.

Horseplay

Kim set up a pony-trekking venture as an activity for holidaymakers with the help of Kathy, who had married Frank's son, Chris, the previous year. However, shortly after the Holiday Village opening, the ponies strayed through an open gate into the road and one had to be destroyed as a result of its injuries.

A war then followed between the Tates and the Sugdens, with Joe seen as a traitor by his own family. Kathy believed that Jack Sugden's son, Robert, was responsible for leaving the gate open, but the boy insisted that he had closed it. Jack pointed out that visitors to the Holiday Village had previously left an Emmerdale gate open, resulting in the organic-fed sheep roaming on to non-organic grass and

At the Country Club's opening, Angharad McAllister gets into the mood of the occasion with male strippers The Nobbies.

becoming technically 'polluted'. As a reprisal, Jack removed signposts that Joe had erected on common footpaths across Emmerdale land, causing inconvenience to holidaymakers.

Seth Armstrong finally cleared Robert's name when he revealed to Jack that he had chased a group of holidaymakers off the game farm and heard them talking about visiting the ponies. Peace was then resumed between the Tates and the Sugdens.

Troubled Teenager

Wayward teenager Lorraine Nelson, daughter of divorced Woolpack barmaid Carol, landed a job at the Holiday Village, where she made a play for both Mark Hughes and Archie Brooks. She also gate-crashed a party staged by Nick Bates and Archie.

Joe Sugden eventually sacked Lorraine and, in an attempt to iron out the teenager's problems, mother Carol persuaded her to move back home with her. The cause of her behaviour turned out to be abuse from her father, Derek.

Heritage Farm Opens

Following the death of tenant farmer George Winslow, Frank planned to turn the buildings and land into a model farm as a visiting attraction for holidaymakers, providing a home for rare breeds of cattle, sheep and pigs. This dream eventually became a reality in 1994, when the heritage farm was opened.

It was not one of the most successfully staged events. The presence of the Dingles, looking for revenge on Luke McAllister's sister, Jessica, and friend Biff Fowler, following the death of Ben Dingle in a fight with Luke, brought an air of menace to the occasion. Also, when the sword dancers booked to perform did not arrive, Frank found them in The Woolpack with a drunken Alan Turner, who was grieving his short-lived second wife, Shirley.

Much worse, Frank ended the day at death's door in hospital after suffering a heart attack. Fortunately, he survived. Seth Armstrong also proved a survivor when he was made heritage farm warden after losing his job as Home Farm gamekeeper to Dave Glover.

A cabin in the Holiday Village is the Cairns family's first residence in Emmerdale.

It was at the heritage farm in 1994 that Frank's daughter, Zoë, started her own veterinary surgery, before switching to Smithy Cottage the following year.

Country Club

Earlier in 1994, Frank agreed to Lynn Whiteley's proposals to set up a country club to attract Holiday Village residents. In an attempt to compete with the refurbished Woolpack, Lynn's grand opening was a ladies' night featuring a group of male exotic dancers, The Nobbies. Their muscles and gyrating bodies proved a hit with the women of Beckindale.

Sarah Connolly and Angharad McAllister were hijacked on to the stage, with a photograph of Angharad and the men – wearing only thongs and bow ties – appearing on the front page of the *Hotten Courier*.

Temporary Home

When the Cairns family – retired Army major Tony, wife Becky, daughters Charlie and Emma, and son Will – arrived in Emmerdale in 1997, they stayed in a Holiday Village cabin while looking for a property to buy.

It was here that Tony and Becky experienced the shock of finding out that 13-year-old Emma was the mother of a new-born baby left outside Zoë Tate's veterinary surgery. Although Tony was intent on baby Geri being adopted and the father being prosecuted, he eventually relented and gave in to Emma's demands to keep her daughter.

After naïvely buying Woodside Farm from Jack Sugden and finding that it needed expensive repairs, the Cairns family rented Tenant House, the cottage owned by Jack's mother, Annie, until the new property was ready for them to move into.

Wishing Well Cottage

1995–   Zak Dingle, Nellie Dingle (1995),
Butch Dingle (1995–), Sam Dingle (1995–6, 1997–),
Tina Dingle (1995–6), Mandy Dingle (1996–),
Marlon Dingle (1996–7), Albert Dingle (1997),
Lisa Clegg (later Dingle) (1997–), Paddy Kirk (1998–)

CREATING REALITY

Five hundred yards from the new Emmerdale village set stands the Dingles' homestead, Wishing Well Cottage, surrounded by pigs and scrap metal. This barn and outbuildings, on the Harewood estate, have been used for both interior and exterior filming since the Dingles were introduced *en masse* to the serial in 1995.

Since shooting began on the new outdoor set, the programme's directors have been able to show it in long shot from the village or give views of the village from Wishing Well Cottage. A former cow byre forms the Dingles' main living accommodation – a combined sitting room, dining room and kitchen.

'When we first came here it had cobbles on the floor, so we had to rip them out and put a concrete floor down to make it safe for the actors,' says designer Mike Long. 'That was also needed to make sure that the cameras, lights and props weren't all wonky.

'Although it still looks pretty tacky, it's in fairly good shape. We also built a fireplace and there's a section from the Woolpack bar that was thrown out when the pub was refurbished in 1995.'

An outbuilding next door provided Uncle Albert and his son, Marlon, with a bedroom before Albert left, Marlon moved to Tenant House and Mandy moved in there with boyfriend Paddy Kirk.

The buildings, in need of work to ensure they remained structurally safe, were improved in the spring of 1998. In the storyline, Lady Tara Oakwell hired builders to do work after Zak was injured inside the former cow byre.

Home Farm supremo Frank Tate found himself in a battle with the Dingles when he tried to evict them from the 19th-century barn and dilapidated outbuildings that had been sublet to the family, rent-free, for more than 20 years by a farmer called Holdgate, one of Frank's tenants on the estate. Following Holdgate's death in 1995, Frank was determined to recover the farmhouse and the farm building next door so that he could rent them to the Glover family.

It came as a shock to him when villagers – including his own son, Chris – showed themselves to be united in support for the Dingles, who had been hated ever since provoking a fight the previous year that ended in Ben Dingle dying and GP's son Luke McAllister facing manslaughter or murder charges – until an eccentric professor contacted by a friend of Luke's father discovered a rare condition that had caused Ben's death.

The Dingle Family – Zak, Nellie and children Sam, Tina and Butch – are hated throughout the village, until Frank Tate tries to evict them.

The Dingles had subsequently mounted a hate campaign against the McAllister family, which contributed to their decision to leave the village. Zak Dingle, a prize fighter in his younger days, had also taken on Ned Glover in a bare-knuckle fight, but his defeat finally ended the campaign of terror that the Dingle clan had waged on the village.

A Dingle's Revenge

Ben's sister, Tina, found a more direct way of exacting callous revenge for Ben's death when she pretended to fall for Luke after his parents' departure. Then she announced that she was pregnant, with the result that Luke proposed to her. Tina's plan was working and, by feigning stomach pains, she subsequently managed to sabotage an important A-level examination that was crucial to his hopes of getting into medical school.

The wedding was planned for 20 July 1995 at St Mary's Church, but Tina jilted Luke at the altar and left the church calmly after telling him that she had never been pregnant. The following month, Luke's devastation led him to bundle Tina into his friend Dave Glover's van and drive off at high speed, before crashing on a bend. Luke died, but Tina escaped and lived to feel remorse for her actions.

Frank's Day of Shame

There were more scenes of bitterness and violence when, in October, the terrible Dingles braced themselves for eviction as the bailiffs moved in. Police were on hand to help them to remove Zak and Nellie Dingle, and their children, Butch, Sam and Tina.

However, such was the strength of local opposition to Frank's action, which villagers saw as an act of injustice by a powerful landlord, that he allowed Zak and his clan to return, at a nominal rent, and gave the Glovers the farmhouse in which Holdgate had previously lived.

Receiving The Woolpack's well as a Valentine's Day gift from Zak after the pub underwent a refurbishment in 1995, Nellie renamed the Dingles' residence Wishing Well Cottage. On the evening of The Woolpack's reopening, Nellie won the raffle, which was drawn by Ian Botham, and a photograph of her with the cricketer found pride of place in her home.

The family also took advantage of the raffle prize – a free meal at the pub – to turn up a week later *en masse*, pointing out that no restriction on numbers had been mentioned. It was a shock to Zak when Nellie left for Ireland at the end of the year to look after her father and never returned.

A Crooked Uncle

Leopards never change their spots, and brothers Butch and Sam teamed up with their crooked Uncle Albert to rob a villain called Kenny Dillon. But they were left to fend for themselves when Albert did a runner and Dillon headed for the Dingles' abode. Tina escaped and met Albert, who gave her the stolen necklace, which she sold to Eric Pollard.

But Tina was then kidnapped by Dillon and held at his mansion, complete with swimming pool, snooker room and champagne flowing constantly. Dillon's aim was to let her go in return for Albert, but such luxury meant that Tina was reluctant to leave when her father arrived to take her home. The police eventually caught up with both Dillon and Albert.

A Woman's Touch

Zak's niece, Mandy Dingle, joined the clan at Wishing Well Cottage in 1996 and teamed up with Tina to help Eric Pollard out by standing in as escorts for an American client. But Tina moved out of the Dingles' homestead to become housekeeper to Frank Tate, who was embroiled in his marital problems with wife Kim.

He was taken with Tina and later made her his personal assistant but, at the end of the year, she walked out on Frank and her own family when he tried to put their relationship on a more personal level.

Zak, pining for Nellie, had woman trouble of his own when he fell for Marilyn. One day, he returned home to discover that she had disappeared with the family's money after tricking them into leaving her alone at Wishing Well Cottage. The Dingles eventually found their van, which she had used as a getaway vehicle, in a hedge.

However, new love came into Zak's life with the arrival of divorcée Lisa Clegg, who dressed in a boiler suit and wellingtons, and was not averse to working for a living, unlike most of the Dingles.

Munching Mandy

Mandy was one Dingle who was prepared to earn her money. She launched Mandy's Munch Box, a mobile burger van, in 1996 but failed to impress a public health inspector when she picked up a burger off the floor. Mandy suffered further when the owners of a rival burger van tried to sabotage the Munch Box and beat her up.

On the romantic front, Mandy seemed doomed. She set her sights on hunky Dave Glover and was thrilled when a blind date was arranged for her after he had ditched lady of the manor Kim Tate. But the evening ended with Mandy being humiliated after Dave dumped her in favour of another woman. She called cousin Butch from a phone box and, in floods of tears, asked him to come to her rescue.

Simple Sam

Sam was always the Dingle most mentally challenged. In 1995, after finding work with Eric Pollard, whose antiques dealings were shady enough already, he performed a house clearance for his boss and moved the contents to Emmerdale village hall, ready for an antiques auction. When Eric discovered that he had cleared 40 Skipdale Road instead of No 14, he ordered Sam to return everything.

The following year, in the course of his period in Pollard's employment, Sam stole a plate from a shop, was arrested, jumped bail and left for Ireland in the back of Lisa's pig van. He stayed there for fear of facing an English court and being jailed, although he made a brief return in May 1997 to act as chauffeur for Pollard and his bride, Dee de la Cruz, in their wedding-day Rolls-Royce – hiding in the nick of time when the police arrived at the reception after a tip-off.

Justice was done when Sam returned for good later in the year and faced a court. Fortunately, he escaped a prison sentence and was able to return home. When Kathy Glover discovered that Sam could not read, she started to teach him.

Enterprising Family

Ensuring a full quota of Dingles at Wishing Well Cottage, Marlon – son of Zak's brother, Albert – arrived in 1996 and showed early signs of entrepreneurial ambitions by suggesting that the family organise a Santa's Grotto in Hotten at Christmas.

There was further Dingle enterprise when Albert arrived with a decrepit bus the following year and suggested starting a local service. The family enraged a rival firm by taking passengers away from it. When they did the same with a school service, the children failed to reach their destination.

However, Lisa made Albert feel at home by converting the outbuilding into a flat for him and Marlon. Lisa's handiwork made her want to take up building as a job and she persuaded the Cairns family to let her do the work that was necessary at Woodside Farm before they could move in.

Even more enterprise was in the air when it was discovered that there was a fortress built on the

Cousin Marlon (right) helps the Dingle clan to organise a money-making Santa's Grotto in Hotten soon after his arrival at Wishing Well Cottage.

Mandy Dingle lures vet Paddy Kirk into her boudoir.

Mandy's Heartbreak

Life seemed to be looking up for Mandy when she landed a job as barmaid at The Woolpack and successfully used her position to chat up vet Paddy Kirk, who was helping out at Zoë Tate's surgery in early 1997. Pub landlord Alan Turner was concerned that his staff should not be chatting up the customers, but non-PC Paddy made it clear that he did not mind.

Mandy was heartbroken when Paddy left for Cumbria after his contract ended. But he returned later in the year and the couple continued where they had left off. Mandy moved into the outbuilding conversion at Wishing Well Cottage in December 1997 and, in the New Year, Paddy moved in with her.

Meanwhile, Marlon – who had found a purpose in life by becoming chef at Pollard's Wine Bar – left the clan and, two months later, joined Biff Fowler at Tenant House.

Butch's Obsession

Butch was having to cope with his own urges when he became obsessed with baby James Tate's nanny, Sophie Wright. She succumbed to his dubious charms by sleeping with him twice after getting drunk, but Butch was unable to cope with the fact that Sophie was having a lesbian relationship with vet Zoë Tate.

After stalking her, taking photographs, making his room a shrine to her and even stealing her nanny's uniform, Butch sent Zoë on a hoax callout and confronted Sophie at Smithy Cottage. He flew into a rage and smashed a photograph of Zoë, but then broke down in tears and made Sophie realise that he was harmless.

Afterwards, father Zak made Butch set light to his pictures of Sophie, called him a filthy pervert and administered a beating with his belt, leaving bruises on Butch's arm.

Wishing Well Cottage Unsafe

Zak satisfied his own desires when he and Lisa finally tied the knot on 28 January 1998. Wishing Well Cottage became a slightly more salubrious place

Dingles' land before the Civil War. Marlon and Butch dug for buried treasure, and Lisa found a sword, although it turned out not to be worth much. However, Zak hit upon the idea of turning Wishing Well Cottage into a medieval museum with a Civil War exhibition that included a guillotine and stocks. After just four people had visited, two Hotten Council officials arrived to inform Zak that he did not have an entertainments licence and the guillotine was lethal. This Dingle project was over.

for the married couple after it became clear that the buildings were unsafe and Lady Tara Oakwell, who had bought a majority shareholding in the Home Farm estate, organised repair work. By then, Lisa had launched a car-repair business in a workshop at Dale Head Farm, near the centre of the village.

Zak finds happiness with Lisa Clegg after seeing first wife Nellie run off to Ireland, never to return.

Holdgate's Farm

1994–8   Ned and Jan Glover, Dave Glover (1994–6),
Linda Glover (later Fowler) (1994–7),
Roy Glover (1994–8), Biff Fowler (1997)

CREATING REALITY

Next to Wishing Well Cottage stands Holdgate's Farm and, in reality, another set that has been used for both interior and exterior filming. It is on the Harewood estate about 500 yards from the village set, which was built two years after this building was first seen in the serial.

The real-life former farmhouse was used as an estate office and a gamekeeper's cottage before lying empty. *Emmerdale* started filming there in 1995, when the Glover family moved in. Behind the farmhouse, production designer Mike Long placed an old tractor and produce from the market garden business that Jan Glover used to run.

The interior had to look a bit faded. 'It appears a bit grotty, which was intentional,' says Mike, 'but it actually looks great on camera. We had to wallpaper the house and then dirty it all down, but the task was to find very old-fashioned wallpaper. You can find it, but you have to have a good eye for what looks old-fashioned.'

The house's bedrooms have also been used for setting scenes in places such as solicitors' offices, and the attic was used as that at Home Farm.

The Glover family's move to Holdgate's Farm, in November 1995, took place more than a year after they became homeless following the sale of their tenant farm on the other side of Robblesfield by a pension fund. Their salvation had been the caravan that father Ned won in a bare-knuckle boxing contest. They adopted it as a home and moved to Emmerdale, where hardworking Ned became a labourer for old friend Jack Sugden while still hoping for his own farm again.

His wife, Jan, backbone of the family, found work behind the bar at The Woolpack, while son Dave, 19, took over from Seth Armstrong as gamekeeper on the Home Farm estate and 16-year-old daughter Linda became Zoë Tate's receptionist at the veterinary surgery. Their younger brother, 13-year-old Roy, was still at school and made friends with Scott Windsor, whose parents had recently bought the village post office.

Date with the Dingles

The Glovers' early days in Emmerdale found them embroiled in the feud between the Dingles and the McAllisters. At a rave party on land owned by Betty Eagleton, Ben Dingle sauntered in without paying, took drinks from Vic Windsor's stall and drove dangerously around the field in his car. No one knew what to do, so Dave Glover decided to take on Ben Dingle by standing in front of his car.

Joe Sugden, knowing of the Dingles' bad reputation, pushed Dave out of the way, hurting the pair of them in the process but preventing much more serious injury. Doctor's daughter Jessica McAllister then beat Ben about the chest, to no effect, and her boyfriend, Biff Fowler, went for Ben but was floored by him, before Ben Dingle took on Jessica's brother, Luke. Just as it looked as if Luke would be given a pasting, Ben fell to the ground unconscious and died.

Ned Glover earns the gratitude of Emmerdale when he beats Zak Dingle in a bare-knuckle fight.

Although it was later found that his death was actually caused by a rare medical condition, the Dingle family – regarded as social outcasts – made life hell for the McAllisters, Glovers and other villagers as they sought revenge.

Ned Strikes a Blow

After Dave and Roy Glover were among those attacked by Butch Dingle and his cronies outside Hotten Comprehensive, Ned found himself in a confrontation with Zak Dingle at The Woolpack that ended in a challenge to a bare-knuckle fight, something in which both men had shown their prowess in the past.

Wife Jan was concerned that Ned's age now counted against him and felt he should no longer resort to violence. He was all set to abandon the fight when daughter Linda revealed that the Dingles had sexually menaced her outside school. This made Ned determined to teach Zak a lesson.

A bloody battle followed, with heavy blows struck by both men, until the pair rolled down an embankment into a stream, where Ned finished the fight with a knockout blow. The Dingles had been tempered and villagers were grateful.

A New Home

When a tenant farmer called Holdgate died on the Home Farm estate in 1995, Frank Tate wanted to take back his farmhouse and the barn and out-buildings next door that the old man had sublet to the Dingles so that he could rent it all out to the Glovers.

Although he succeeded in evicting the Dingles, such was the outcry of villagers – who found one reason to support the Dingle clan in Frank's use of power in making a family homeless – that the lord of the manor capitulated and let the Dingles move back into their outbuildings while the Glovers moved into the farmhouse.

Heartache for Linda

Shortly before moving to Holdgate's Farm, the family had suffered another crisis. Linda fell for handsome Danny Weir, who turned out to be the son of wealthy Lady Weir. He even invited her for a weekend in Amsterdam, but Linda found out that she was being used after reading in a society magazine that Danny was engaged to aristocratic Libbis Foster-Cuthbert.

When Linda discovered she was pregnant, she aborted the baby by injecting herself with horse tranquillisers that she found in Zoë's veterinary surgery. As a result she collapsed and ended up fighting for her life in hospital.

On finding out what had happened, Linda's father thundered over to Lady Weir's mansion and threw Danny into the swimming pool. As he jumped in to finish the job, with fists flying, son Dave arrived to stop Ned doing further damage.

Dave's Doomed Affair

Dave Glover also played with fire through his choice of women in Emmerdale. After he tried to get close to Kathy Tate, her husband Chris, from whom she had recently separated, was furious to hear that his father, Frank, had appointed Dave assistant farm manager at Home Farm.

It was Frank's turn to question that appointment when Dave had an affair with his wife, Kim. But the couple kept the secret from him for months,

At Dave Glover's funeral, emotions run high between his widow Kathy and lover Kim.

Jan's Misery

The Glovers' miserable 1996 had been exacerbated when Jan set up a fruit-and-veg stall in a lay-by to earn money and was set upon by a gang of thugs. As the family's debts mounted, Jan started dipping into the till at The Woolpack and was sacked by Alan Turner when he caught her.

Following the death of her son Dave, Kim Tate's return to Home Farm and the death of Kim's husband Frank, Jan became housekeeper at Home Farm, complete with a uniform that was designed to ensure she knew her place. Kim gave her employment because Jan believed herself to be the grandmother of Kim's baby, James, never accepting the results of blood tests that confirmed that Frank was the real father. However, Jan consistently showed disapproval for James's nanny, Sophie Wright, who had begun a lesbian relationship with Zoë Tate.

during which time Frank even gave Dave a bonus for all his good work.

Dave then dumped Kim, proposed to Kathy and moved into the flat above her tearooms. When she discovered that he was seeing Kim again, Kathy called off the engagement. Although Dave eventually married Kathy, in November 1996, he planned to leave Emmerdale the following month with Kim and baby James, whom he mistakenly believed to be his son.

Tragically, Dave died after rescuing James from the nursery at Home Farm during a fire. It was the first of several tragedies to befall the Glover family.

True Romance

More happily, it appeared that Linda had found true romance when she started going out with Dave's friend, Biff Fowler, who had previously dated both Dolores Sharp and Jessica McAllister – and taken their virginity.

After she moved in with Biff in a cottage on the Home Farm estate – where Biff had been made estate manager – the couple married on 24 December 1996. Following the tragedy of Dave's death, they moved back to Holdgate's Farm to live with Linda's grieving parents and the marriage that looked to be made in heaven began with a grim shadow hanging over it.

Emmerdale's young lovers, Linda Glover and Biff Fowler, tie the knot, but their wedding night comes to an abrupt end with the news that Linda's brother, Dave, has suffered fatal injuries in a fire at Home Farm.

Whose Baby?

Baby business continued to preoccupy the Glovers. Discovering a mystery baby dumped in a box outside Zoë Tate's veterinary surgery – who turned out to be the daughter of 13-year-old Emma Cairns – made Linda broody and she told Biff of her longing to have a child.

The course of events that followed made 1997 just as full of tragedy for the Glover family as the previous year had been. Biff's mother, Sandra Fowler, had tried to prevent her son going ahead with his wedding by telling him that his estranged father, Ron Hudson, had developed Huntington's disease, which is hereditary. At the time, Biff believed this was simply a ruse to deny him happiness with Linda.

However, in May 1997, Ron died from the disease and Biff was told that if he fathered any children he might not live long enough to see them grow up and they could have defective genes themselves. Linda then confirmed that she was pregnant.

Unable to give his news to Linda, Biff sought advice from Kathy Glover, who persuaded him to take a test to see whether he was in fact carrying the disease. He finally confided in Linda, who believed that she was now being punished for aborting Danny Weir's baby.

Further tragedy strikes the Glover family when Linda dies in a car crash with Lord Alex Oakwell at the wheel.

In his darkest hour, Biff contemplated suicide by jumping off a viaduct. Fortunately, young Andy Hopwood was passing and talked him out of it. Biff and Linda were relieved when the test for Huntington's disease proved negative. But Linda was distraught when she miscarried in July 1997.

Biff's Heartbreak

Worse was to follow when Linda and Biff attended Kim Tate and Steve Marchant's engagement party on 21 October. Kim encouraged Lord Alex Oakwell, drugged up on cocaine, to make a play for Linda, who had rowed with Biff. Linda left the party with the aristocrat, who drove away in Steve's Porsche and crashed it into a tree. Before leaving the scene, he moved Linda into the driver's seat. Alex then fled the country, with his wife, Tara, and Kim covering up for him.

While tackling his grief, Biff had a one-night stand with 16-year-old Kelly Windsor, who became pregnant but sought a means of getting an abortion by seducing her boss, Chris Tate, and claiming that he was the father. Chris proved keen for her to have the baby, but Kelly miscarried after falling down the stairs at Home Farm following a skirmish with Kim.

James Goes Missing

The affairs of the Glovers and Tates were intertwined again when, in December 1997, Kim's young son, James, went missing. The kidnapper turned out to be Jan, who was found with the boy at St Mary's Maternity Hospital in Hotten – where her own son Dave had been born – talking to him as if he were her dead son years earlier.

No charges were made against Jan, but she was sent to hospital for psychiatric treatment under the Mental Health Act and Ned and Roy found her state of mind difficult to understand. Eventually, Jan left her husband and son to start a new life away from Emmerdale with her sister, June Worel.

Ned and Roy also faced the prospect of looking for somewhere new to live in 1998 after they were evicted from Holdgate's Farm, victims of an asset-stripping exercise by Home Farm's new lady of the manor, Tara Oakwell.

Jan, unable to cope with the loss of two of her children, kidnaps baby James Tate and ends up in a psychiatric hospital.

St Mary's Church

Vicarage		**Subsequent clergy**
1972–6	Revd Edward and Liz Ruskin	**(not living in vicarage):**
1977	Revd William Hockley,	1990–1 Tony Charlton (curate)
	Revd David Cowper	1991–3 Revd Jackson
1977–89	Revd Donald Hinton	1994 Revd Richards
Lodgers:	Alison Gibbons (1973),	1995–6 Revd Burns
	Dolly Skilbeck (1977),	1996– Revd Ashley Thomas
	Clive Hinton (1978),	
	Jackie Merrick (1982),	
	Barbara Peters (1983)	

CREATING REALITY

Although no church was built on the Harewood set, there is a churchyard full of gravestones, some of them for characters who have died in the serial. It is situated near the vet's surgery, a short distance from the stream, which is crossed by a bridge. A small war memorial stands opposite the churchyard, and the village hall is not far away.

'I ensured all the gravestones were facing south,' says designer Mike Long, 'so that light would hit the stones when we film there. There's a lovely view from the bridge, looking through the churchyard and up to the village.'

The headstones came from a huge cemetery in the East End of London, which was being partially cleared in order to create much-needed building land.

The first two great loves of Kim Marchant's life are buried in the churchyard. First husband Frank Tate's grand headstone is positioned just behind that of her tragic lover Dave Glover. Ben Dingle's grave is marked with a wooden cross.

St Mary's Church has been featured in *Emmerdale* from the first episode and Mike hopes that he will eventually be given the budget to build it at Harewood. Until then, any church scenes will be filmed on location. They were previously shot at St Paul's Church, Esholt, whose vicarage was also used for filming during the days when Emmerdale had its own parish priest.

St Mary's Church has been the setting for many weddings, funerals and baptisms down the years in Emmerdale. Originally, the Saxons had a wooden church on the site, but it was rebuilt in stone by the Normans. Although parts of that work remain, going back to the year AD 989, the rest is Victorian Gothic, added after a fire in 1882 believed to have been started by a choirboy who had been banned from the church for smoking in the vestry.

The church contains the tombs of the early de Verniers, who as the Verneys became the squires of Beckindale. The nearby vicarage, a spacious Georgian manse, was often host to village fêtes until the retirement of the parish's last vicar, the Revd Donald Hinton, in 1989.

Cradle to Grave

Back in October 1972, when Annie Sugden's husband, Jacob, was laid to rest in the churchyard, the Revd Edward Ruskin was the parish of Beckindale and Demdale's vicar. Over the next few years, he was to bury Annie's daughter, Peggy, following an aneurysm, and her grandchildren, Sam and Sally, after a train hit them in a stalled car on a level crossing.

The twins, barely three years old, had been baptised by the Revd Ruskin, who was a source of great comfort to the Sugden family in the aftermath of these tragic events and knew he had a great ally in Annie's father, Sam Pearson, whose belief in God was unshakeable. However, the vicar's conversations with Jack made even him question some aspects of his faith.

More happily, in March 1973, the vicar married blacksmith Frank Blakey and Janie Harker, sister of Pat Merrick, the divorcée who later wed Jack Sugden in a register office. He also officiated at the wedding of Joe Sugden and Christine Sharp in 1974, which saw the men wearing top hats and morning suits – apart from Sam Pearson, who obstinately refused. Unfortunately, the marriage lasted only five weeks. The following year, Annie Sugden became a churchwarden.

During 1973, widow Alison Gibbons – whom Edward had previously known in Liverpool – came to stay at the vicarage in an attempt to get over the death of her husband and child in a car crash.

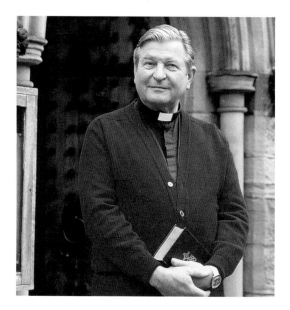

The Revd Donald Hinton arrives in 1977 and becomes Beckindale's longest-serving vicar.

Alison worked as a barmaid at The Woolpack before becoming an assistant at the village shop, whose premises she subsequently owned with Henry Wilks and lived in. After her departure in 1974, Edward's wife, Liz, took a part-time job at the shop when Henry was looking for someone to help.

Two years later, the Ruskins left Beckindale and there was a break before the Revd William Hockley, a bicycle-riding former missionary in Africa, became the new incumbent in 1977. His stay was short and, before the year was out, he was replaced first by the Revd David Cowper, then by the Revd Donald Hinton, who became Beckindale's longest-serving vicar in living memory, remaining there until his retirement in 1989.

Long-serving Vicar

During David Cowper's tenure at the vicarage, he had allowed Dolly Skilbeck to stay there after her arrival from Darlington to work as a barmaid at The Woolpack. She had been hired by Henry Wilks as a live-in barmaid, but Amos Brearly had other ideas and she moved out.

On widower Donald's arrival, she found new accommodation at Emmerdale Farm, where she fell for labourer Matt Skilbeck, and the couple's wedding in June 1978 was the new vicar's first in the village, with Dolly wearing a dress of oyster silk.

With Jack Sugden and Pat Merrick's wedding taking place at Hotten Register Office, it was ten years before Donald had another wedding in the church, when Jackie Merrick married Kathy Bates. The bride wore Annie Sugden's Edwardian gown – also worn by Annie's mother – after a burst water pipe resulted in her own wedding dress being destroyed on the eve of the ceremony.

At a time of very few births in the village, Donald – who was known as a good listener and a collector of books and butterflies – baptised Matt and Dolly's son, Sam, in 1983 and Jack and Pat's son, Robert, three years later. Joe Sugden returned from France just in time to attend his nephew's baptism.

However, Robert's birth was followed in August 1986 by the tragic death of Pat in a car crash and she was buried in the churchyard. Just two years earlier, Donald had officiated at the funeral of Sam Pearson, who was much missed by daughter Annie and her clan.

Donald surprised villagers in April 1989 by agreeing to marry divorcées Joe Sugden and Kate Hughes, but Kate was a regular churchgoer who had wed her first husband in a register office, so their vows had not been exchanged in front of God. It proved to be the vicar's last wedding before his retirement that summer.

During his time in the parish, Donald had also been responsible for organising dog races, planning horticultural shows and heading Beckindale's bid to win the Best Kept Village in the Dales competition, which was thwarted when rivals dumped horse manure in the forecourt of The Woolpack.

Close to Home

In Donald's occasional absences, services were taken by the Revd Bob Jerome and, once or twice, the returning Edward Ruskin. In 1981, before marrying Jack Sugden, Pat Merrick became the vicar's housekeeper and, the following year, the Revd Bill Jeffries was appointed as assistant minister, but his laid-back style ensured that his stay was short. Donald also became rural dean in 1982 but, staying loyal to his flock, refused the opportunity to become an archdeacon because it would have taken him away from his parishioners.

Another guest at the vicarage in 1982 was Pat's son, Jackie Merrick, who agreed to stay there as a condition of bail on being charged with setting fire to his NY Estates caravan after being sacked as assistant gamekeeper.

Donald had problems with his own children during his time in Beckindale. Just a year after his arrival, son Clive came on a visit before being arrested in Athens for gun-running. Then, in 1983, Donald's daughter, Barbara Peters, left her philandering husband Brian, moved into the vicarage and took a job as secretary to NY Estates manager Alan Turner at Home Farm.

Trying to engineer a reconciliation, Donald fixed up a meeting with husband Brian, but Barbara stormed out and moved in with Joe Sugden at 3 Demdyke Row. She started off in the spare room, but friendship turned to passion. Donald disapproved and Barbara eventually left Joe, sparing her father's feelings by telling him she was returning to her husband while promising Joe that she was not.

More dramatically, Donald was held at gunpoint by Derek Warner in 1986 after the crook had fallen out with partner-in-crime Harry Mowlem over the proceeds of a security van robbery. Fortunately, no one was hurt and Warner was taken away by the police.

Vicarless Parish

The village has not had its own vicar since Donald's retirement in 1989 and the vicarage has not been inhabited. Services have been held in rotation with three other village churches, and various curates and rectors have taken services at St Mary's.

A year after Donald's departure, curate Tony Charlton arrived from London shortly after being ordained and stayed in a small cottage leased by Hotten Parish Council. He proved to be the only permanent incumbent, but his stay was short.

One of Tony's first tasks, in August 1990, was to officiate at the funeral of Pete Whiteley, who had tragically died when Kate Sugden accidentally ran him over following his affair with her teenage daughter, Rachel.

He befriended Kate and acted as a character witness for her in court. However, the prosecution counsel portrayed Tony as a gauche, impressionable young man and she was convicted of manslaughter.

As Kate served 12 months of a two-year sentence, Tony was a regular prison visitor. Through him, Kate – riddled with guilt – informed husband Joe that she did not want him to see her, something he found difficult to accept.

Tony himself left for London in 1991 after becoming infatuated with young widow Kathy Merrick before she married Chris Tate in a register-office ceremony.

Saddest Day

Increasingly, weddings have taken place at Hotten Register Office, especially as divorcées such as Alan Turner and Chris Tate married again. Unbeknown to his bride, Elizabeth Feldmann, and to villagers, Eric Pollard was already married when the pair exchanged vows at St Mary's Church in October 1992.

One service entirely appropriate in the village church was when widow Annie Sugden married wealthy businessman Leonard Kempinski in October 1993, but it did not go without incident. The Revd Jackson was due to take the service, but he lost his voice and handed over to Donald Hinton, who was attending as a guest.

Just three months later, St Mary's Church was witness to the saddest day in its long history as the victims of the plane disaster – Archie Brooks, Elizabeth Pollard, Mark Hughes and Leonard Kempinski – were buried. The Revd Richards officiated at the funeral service.

Other funerals in recent years have included those of Shirley Turner, who was shot dead by a gunman after a raid on the village post office went wrong, Joe Sugden, who was killed in a car crash in Spain in 1995, Dave Glover, who died after rescuing Kim Tate's baby from a blazing Home Farm in 1996, and millionaire landowner Frank Tate, who died of a heart attack the following year.

The Village Institute

Below *Britt Woods and Viv Windsor wipe the smile off their husbands' faces when they step in for strippers booked by Vic and Terry at a sportsmen's dinner.*

Down the years, the village institute – built for the community by the Verney family – has been the scene of many events that have brought the people of Emmerdale together. Home-made entertainment has often been the order of the day, with plays and pantomimes performed there.

Publican Amos Brearly was a leading light on stage, playing Dame Margery in a 1978 production of *Jack and the Beanstalk* that also featured Joe Sugden and Dolly Acaster. He took starring roles in *The Pirates of Penzance* in 1984, with a cast that included Seth Armstrong, Dolly Skilbeck, Jackie Merrick and Sgt Ian MacArthur, and a 1990 performance of *Dracula*, which he wrote as a serious drama but proved to be a great comic success.

In the same year, Kathy Merrick wowed everyone in the hall with her performance of a song called 'Just This Side of Love', written by husband-to-be Chris Tate – secretly recorded by him and later heard by an astonished Kathy on The Woolpack's jukebox.

CREATING REALITY

The village institute is one of a handful of sets filmed inside and out at Harewood. Designer Mike Long based the building on the one previously used at Esholt but made a few modifications.

'The previous location was pebbledash render, but I've gone for a timber-frame construction with stone porch,' he says. 'I've also given it a green slate roof so that it's different from the other roofs.

'In Esholt, they put a suspended ceiling inside, presumably because it's expensive to heat. Here, I designed it how Esholt would have been, with a lovely, high, beamed ceiling. I've moved the kitchen – it was on the left as you entered through the main doors, but now it is opposite you – and I've built a verandah at the back, overlooking the stream.'

The location of the village hall has been changed, too. Previously, it was at the end of the main street on the left, roughly where The Mill is currently positioned. At Harewood, Mike planned the building in a more central position, behind the post office and between the churchyard and tearooms (now a diner).

There is a car park in front of the hall, on the land between it and the terrace that includes the cottages inhabited by Kathy Glover and Betty Eagleton and Seth Armstrong. A playground, with swings, slide and seesaw provided by Bradford Metropolitan Council, is positioned between the hall and the tearooms.

More Serious Matters

Politics entered Beckindale life when a public meeting was called at the village hall in 1987 to discuss the government's plans to site an underground nuclear waste dump at nearby Pencross Fell. This meeting established villagers' unity against the proposal, despite local MP Harriet Ridgley-Jones speaking in favour of it, and the fight was eventually won.

Strippers and Dancers

In 1995, the hall was the setting for the Emmerdale sportsmen's dinner, when rascals Terry Woods and Vic Windsor booked strippers as the entertainment. When their wives, Britt and Viv, found out about this, they soon wiped the smiles off the pair's faces by standing in for the strippers, walking off the stage and throwing bucketsful of water over their husbands.

The following year, when Viv Windsor decided she wanted to take dancing lessons at the village hall, she failed to persuade Vic to join her. Terry was willing to step in, though – and to start an affair with the postmistress.

Stolen Property

The village hall was also the venue for an antiques auction organised by Eric Pollard and Terry Woods in 1995. Stolen property ended up there after Sam Dingle undertook a house clearance but entered the wrong cottage. As a result, Pollard ordered him to return the furniture.

Pollard was also responsible for convening a meeting at the village hall in the same year to rally villagers against Frank Tate's attempts to evict the Dingles from a barn and outbuilding sublet to them free by a farmer called Holdgate, who had died that year. Eventually, Frank let them stay, but charged rent.

Three years later, the rector, the Revd Ashley Thomas, ordered Pollard to move antiques that he had stockpiled there. When he failed to do so, Ashley put them up for sale at £5 an item, so Pollard moved everything into Farrers Barn, from where he conducted his business.

Cricket Pavilion

Opposite *Joe Sugden and brother-in-law Matt Skilbeck enjoy the village's annual cricket match against Robblesfield.*

The annual cricket match against neighbouring Robblesfield, played on the field donated to the community by the Verney family, is a village tradition dating back to 1903, with both teams playing to win the Butterworth Ball. The event has been the centre of controversy more than once.

In 1977, Robblesfield included in its team Phil Kitson, a former professional cricketer, and his bowling skills left Beckindale 28 all out after they went in to bat. Then, as Robblesfield prepared to bat, fortune looked down on the home team. A siren called its firemen from the field to an emergency and the match had to be abandoned. As a result, a coin was tossed and Beckindale won!

Beckindale's team chairman, Sam Pearson, was horrified when it was discovered that the Butterworth Ball had been stolen from The Woolpack. To save face, he replaced it with an old one of his own, but was presented with an awkward situation when Fred Teaker, licensee of The Miller's Arms in Robblesfield, asked to borrow the ball to display for the team's bicentenary.

It emerged that Teaker's brother had stolen the ball and thrown it into the vicarage garden in Beckindale. A search there by Sam with Woolpack owners Amos Brearly and Henry Wilks yielded nothing. They then found out that the village scout troop had cleared the garden the day after the theft and the vicar had given the ball to young Billy Luttercombe, who found it. Unfortunately, he had lost it in the village allotments.

Sam's daughter, Annie Sugden, finally solved the mystery when she arrived at The Woolpack with the ball, which Willie Ockroyd had found in his cold frame and tossed into a bag for the village jumble sale.

In 1981, the villagers organised a cricket match between Beckindale and NY Estates, which had bought Home Farm from the Verney family three years earlier. The aim was to raise money for the local playgroup, where Dolly Skilbeck worked.

The village cricket team began to benefit from younger blood in the 1990s. However, the 1994 match against Robblesfield was hit by the absence

CREATING REALITY

Across the stream from the churchyard, a cricket pavilion is sited on the edge of the village green. The green is too steep to play a realistic game of cricket, but designer Mike Long commissioned 'a bit of careful levelling' during the summer of 1998 to make it suitable to film a match there if required. 'The pavilion was designed so that it could be filmed from the footbridge over the stream,' says Mike, 'or, if we're shooting along the verandah, we can see the village in the background.'

of Bernard McAllister and his son Luke, who was languishing in a prison cell after being charged with manslaughter following the death of Ben Dingle. Frank Tate, in the middle of his battle with the bottle as a result of his marriage problems, also had to withdraw from the team, as did Alan Turner, who made last-minute excuses following a drinking bout as he sank to the depths of despair following his wife Shirley's tragic death.

Emmerdale team captain Seth Armstrong played his trump card by enlisting the services of Samson the horse first to trample the wicket so that it was unplayable, then to race off with the match ball in his mouth. The final straw came with the discovery that the match trophy, a barrel of beer, had mysteriously been emptied, and the match was called off.

Hotten

Hotten Market is the scene of many of
Eric Pollard's dodgy dealings in the late
1980s after he steps in as manager and
head auctioneer, but auctioneer Sandie
Merrick spots him cooking the books.

Hotten, 7½ miles from Emmerdale, is a town with a produce market, cattle market, police station, council offices, register office, comprehensive school and local newspaper, as well as a cinema, theatre, art gallery, weaving museum and restaurants. Many villagers travel there to shop or enjoy an evening out, although its offerings are more subdued than those in far-flung Leeds and Bradford.

Recorded in the Domesday Book, Hotten – whose name means 'farm on the ridge' – boasts panoramic views over Wharfedale and has been inhabited for more than a thousand years. The weekly open-air produce market was established by Royal Charter in 1110 by Henry I and has taken place every Friday since the Middle Ages. Pat Merrick took a job as a waitress at the market café after leaving first husband Tom and returning to Beckindale in 1980.

Hotten Market, where cattle are sold, also dates back to the 12th century, when Dales sheep breeders trekked there to sell and buy their animals and to trade their wool. Auctioneer James Price handled the sale of the Verney family's estate in Beckindale to NY Estates in 1978.

Seven years later, Karen Moore became an auctioneer. When, in 1986, Joe Sugden became regional manager of NY Estates, the company bought the market from Arthur Golding, whose family had owned it for three generations. The aim was to add the marketing side of farming to NY's activities. Joe also found romance with Karen Moore.

When Karen left her job as assistant auctioneer, Sandie Merrick stepped in. Then, Eric Pollard, brought in as manager of the market and head auctioneer in 1987, turned out to be a crook who fiddled the books and privately sold some of the antiques placed for auction. Sandie reported Pollard's deeds to Joe, who sacked him.

After Sandie took over his position, Pollard mounted a hate campaign against her. However, the market was closed before the end of the year – and earmarked for demolition – when NY Estates decided to pull out after its brief venture in Hotten. When it was reopened by Hotten District Council

Scenes set in Hotten have always been filmed in the historic market town of Otley, celebrated for its cobbled market square and old buttercross, where farmers' wives once sold butter and eggs.

As well as filming at Otley cattle market, *Emmerdale* has used the town's main street for many sequences, such as when the Dingles set up a Christmas shop. A wine bar called Corks has also been featured many times.

In recent years, weddings set in Hotten Register Office have been filmed in Harrogate, including those between Eric Pollard and Dee de la Cruz, and Zak Dingle and Lisa Clegg.

two years later, Pollard was back at the helm, thanks to his collusion with crooked councillor Charlie Aindow, chairman of the markets committee. The police never caught up with Aindow.

Emmerdale once had its own police station, built in 1856 and opened by the Mayor of Hotten, but this became a private house when the village started being policed from Hotten. PC Ted Edwards kept an eye on Beckindale between 1977 and 1980, when kindly Sgt MacArthur took over. He had to deal with a spate of robberies and the spectacle of villagers protesting against government plans for a nuclear waste dump nearby.

Emmerdale comes under the jurisdiction of Hotten Council, which provides many of its services. These included a mobile library, run by librarian Sarah Connolly, until the service was axed in 1990 as a result of budget cuts.

But councillors such as Charlie Aindow and Daniel Hawkins have not portrayed local government in its best light. As well as his dealings with Eric Pollard, Aindow had an affair with Dolly Skilbeck, ending with her having an abortion after falling pregnant. Later, Dawkins teamed up with Pollard in an attempt to make money by buying land and campaigning for the building of an open prison on it.

Hotten Register Office has been used increasingly by Emmerdale residents in recent times. Jack Sugden and Pat Merrick took their vows there in 1982 after the village's vicar, Donald Hinton, refused to marry the couple in church because Pat had been divorced. Alan Turner, also a divorcé, wed Shirley Foster there in February 1994. Jack Sugden married his second wife, Sarah Connolly, in the Register Office three months later and Chris Tate and Rachel Hughes chose it the following year as a quiet venue for their wedding, away from Chris's interfering father, Frank.

Most Emmerdale schoolchildren over 11 attend Hotten Comprehensive. Unfortunately, it has occasionally been the scene of violence, such as when the Dingles attacked Luke McAllister and Biff Fowler outside following Ben Dingle's death in a fight with Luke. Inside, troubled youngster Andy Hopwood even hit teacher Miss Cullen, leading to his exclusion from class.

The *Hotten Courier*, a local newspaper established in 1760, appointed Woolpack landlord Amos Brearly as its part-time Beckindale correspondent after Percy Edgar's death in 1976. The sight of Amos cycling around the village looking for news became familiar.

During the 1980s, Henry Braithwaite's veterinary practice employed Ruth Pennington, who found romance with Joe Sugden as a result of her calls at Home Farm before returning to her fiancé, a wealthy horse breeder, in Ireland. In the following decade, Zoë Tate worked for Martin Bennett's veterinary practice after finishing her exams. She quit in 1991 after discovering that it was carrying out experiments on animals and later set up her own practice in Emmerdale.

The annual Hotten Show demonstrated the changes back in the village when, in 1992, Jack Sugden's wife-to-be, Sarah Connolly, baked a carrot cake that won first prize in its class and beat his mother Annie – a frequent past winner – into second place.

Kim Tate fell and broke her leg in the showjumping competition as young Robert Sugden took part in the junior event for the first time after having riding tuition from Kathy Tate. A tug-of-war between The Woolpack and Frank Tate's Holiday Village team ended inconclusively, with angry exchanges. Meanwhile, judge Alan Turner was faced with the dilemma of choosing between Caroline Bates and Elizabeth Feldmann – both former employees – in the Glamorous Grannie competition. After much soul-searching and embarrassment, he chose Elizabeth.

Kindly Sgt MacArthur waits until after Elizabeth Feldmann's wedding to Eric Pollard to arrest Michael Feldmann for his part in a robbery at Home Farm in 1992.

Locations Past

Inglebrook becomes the home of Henry Wilks and daughter Marian after their arrival in Beckindale in 1972.

INGLEBROOK

1972–3   Henry Wilks, Marian Wilks

Retired Bradford wool merchant Henry Wilks bought Inglebrook in 1972, shortly after the death of his wife, and moved in with his daughter, Marian. She left the following January, heading off for a Greek islands cruise but ending up in New Zealand and, later, Rome. Henry's time in Inglebrook was cut short by a blaze in April 1973 caused by a red-hot cinder falling out of the open fire on to the rug. After a short stay at Emmerdale Farm, Henry moved in at The Woolpack before buying the pub in partnership with landlord Amos Brearly.

HAWTHORN COTTAGE
(See also *Emmerdale Farm: Farmhouse 2*, page 33)

1972   Henry Wilks (not resident)
1973   Matt and Peggy Skilbeck,
             Sam and Sally Skilbeck
1974–7   Joe and Christine Sugden (1974)

Joe and Christine Sugden move into Hawthorn Cottage following their 1974 wedding, but she moves out after only five weeks.

Henry Wilks beat Jack Sugden to buying old Harry Jameson's stone farmhouse and 50-acre smallholding adjoining Emmerdale Farm in 1972. After the birth of twins Sam and Sally the following April, Matt and Peggy Skilbeck moved in and renamed the house Hawthorn Cottage – after an adjacent hawthorn wood. Just three months later, Peggy died tragically of a subarachnoid haemorrhage.

In 1974, Joe and Christine Sugden began married life at Hawthorn Cottage after honeymooning in London, but Christine walked out on Joe after five weeks. They were later divorced and Joe lived in the house on his own until selling it in 1977, buying 3 Demdyke Row and moving in there with new lover Kathy Gimbel.

Hawthorn Cottage returned to the Sugden family in 1993, when Jack and Sarah bought it in a dilapidated condition from Bob Thorley. Subsidence had forced them to leave their original farmhouse, so they moved in and renamed it Emmerdale. However, it was bulldozed four years later to make way for an access road to Demdyke Quarry.

Joe Sugden and Kathy Gimbel find a love-nest at 3 Demdyke Row.

3 DEMDYKE ROW

1977–83	Joe Sugden, Kathy Gimbel (1977), Jackie Merrick (1982), Barbara Peters (1983)
1984–6	Jackie Merrick
1986–8	Joe Sugden, Phil Pearce and Sandie Merrick (1986)
1988–90	Jackie (1988–9) and Kathy Merrick, Nick Bates (1989–93)
1990	Nick Bates, Archie Brooks (both squatting)
1990–3	Nick Bates, Elsa Feldmann (1990–1), Kathy Merrick (1991), Alice Bates, Archie Brooks (both 1992–3)

Percy Edgar, who lived at 3 Demdyke Row, was Beckindale correspondent for the *Hotten Courier* until his death in 1976. The following year, Joe Sugden bought his house and moved in with Kathy Gimbel. Because both were still married, their affair scandalised the village. The pressure of this situation, and her father's subsequent suicide, led to Kathy leaving both Joe and Beckindale.

After a period by himself at the cottage, Joe was joined there in 1983 by the Revd Donald Hinton's married daughter, Barbara Peters, but she too walked out on him. He then left for France and a job breeding Charollais cattle on an NY Estates beef ranch.

When Joe returned from France in 1986 to become NY Estates regional manager, he moved back into his cottage. Unable to get on with Joe, Jackie Merrick, who had been staying there in his absence, went back to the farm and began a romance with Kathy Bates that led to their marriage. For a short time, lovers Phil Pearce and Sandie Merrick lodged with Joe before moving to The Mill.

After NY Estates bought Hotten Market, Joe fell for auctioneer Karen Moore, who had previously had an affair with Joe's brother, Jack. Her romance with Joe fizzled out. He had little more luck with well-heeled vet Ruth Pennington, whom he met in

1987 during her visits to Home Farm. They had in common a love of horses and horse-riding, but Ruth dumped him the following year to return to her fiancé, a wealthy horse breeder in Ireland named Liam.

Joe returned to Emmerdale Farm and Jackie and Kathy Merrick moved into the cottage in December 1988, having started their married life in the attic at Emmerdale Farm the previous February. But they were to spend less than a year together in the cottage – until Jackie's tragic death in August 1989 after accidentally shooting himself while hunting a fox for a £10 bet.

This came shortly after Kathy had experienced a miscarriage as a result of contracting a rare virus from a sheep she was tending while working at Emmerdale Farm. Her brother, Nick Bates, lived with her in the house for a while.

Dolly Skilbeck bought the cottage from Joe in 1990 while working as live-in housekeeper for Frank Tate at Home Farm. Joe suspected that Dolly was having an affair with Frank and using the house as a love-nest, but it emerged that she had bought the cottage as an investment.

After Nick Bates and Archie Brooks started squatting there in 1990, Dolly agreed to rent the cottage out to Nick and his fiancée, Elsa Feldmann. However, their Valentine's Day register-office wedding never went ahead owing to the premature birth of daughter Alice. Elsa and Nick grew further apart and, just before Christmas, she walked out on him and left for Leeds.

But Elsa returned the baby to Nick in the New Year after resenting the commitment of being a mother. Nick proved a good father to Alice, with some help from sister Kathy, who moved in with him for a short time before her wedding to Chris Tate. Archie Brooks also helped out with looking after Alice, and in 1992 he moved back to the cottage as a full-time childminder.

Tragedy followed in December 1993 when Archie was killed as a plane crashed over Beckindale and fireballs shot down from the sky, destroying the cottage. The survival of Alice, discovered alive in the rubble, was considered a miracle.

Seth Armstrong lives with wife Meg at 6 Demdyke Row until her death in 1993 and the destruction of the cottage in the plane crash shortly afterwards.

6 DEMDYKE ROW

1978–93   Seth and Meg Armstrong,
Fred and Jimmy Armstrong
(both 1978–9)

Seth Armstrong, an odd-job man at Connelton Primary School, lived at 6 Demdyke Row with his wife, Meg, and sons Fred and Jimmy until they left home. He had been illiterate, but was taught to read and write by teacher Antony Moeketsi. Then, as Beckindale's wiliest poacher, he was the perfect choice for the job when new NY Estates manager Maurice Westrop hired him as gamekeeper at Home Farm in 1979.

Villagers rarely saw Meg as she stayed at home while Seth propped up the bar of The Woolpack, latterly owned by Alan Turner, who with Frank Tate was one of his two employers following the selling of the Home Farm estate and the break-up of the fish and game farm into two businesses.

However, Seth was devastated when he returned home one day in February 1993 to find Meg dead. Just ten months later, he lost his home too, when Demdyke Row was destroyed as a result of the plane crash, along with his beloved dog, Smokey.

On the night of the disaster, Seth's disappearance caused grave concern, but fears for the worst proved unfounded when he reappeared in the village and revealed that he had found refuge with widowed old flame Betty Eagleton. The couple later moved into Keepers Cottage together.

HOLLY FARM

1975–7	Jim and Freda Gimbel, Kathy Gimbel, Martin Gimbel, Davy Gimbel
1978	Winn and Nicky Groves

Tenant farmer Jim Gimbel was a tyrant who ruled his family – wife Freda, daughter Kathy and sons Martin and Davy – with a rod of iron. Freda was a good friend of Annie Sugden and the pair belonged to the local Women's Institute and visited Hotten Market together.

The lives of the two families became more intertwined when Annie Sugden's son Joe started dating Kathy after she had walked out on her husband, Terry Davis. Kathy had been forced into marriage by her father when she became pregnant, but she miscarried, left her husband and returned to Holly Farm. Then, in 1977, she moved into 3 Demdyke Row with Joe and caused a scandal in the village. When Joe told Jim that they would marry once their divorces were through, he was thrown out of the farmhouse.

Tyrannical farmer Jim Gimbel and wife Freda live with friction and bitterness at Holly Farm.

Meanwhile, Rosemary Kendall, the teenage daughter of Annie's cousin who was staying at Emmerdale Farm, started seeing Martin Gimbel, who worked on the smallholding for a pittance. Rosemary later returned to her mother in Middlesbrough and Martin left home to join the Army.

After Jim raised his hand to younger son Davy, who had dared to defend his sister, wife Freda walked out on him and headed for Leeds. Jim then killed himself with a shotgun. This was too much for Kathy, who was racked with guilt and left Joe and Beckindale to start a new life in Hotten.

Winn and Nicky Groves later moved into Holly Farm, whose ownership passed from the Verneys to NY Estates when the property conglomerate moved into the village.

Enoch Tolly comes into conflict with wife Grace at Tolly Farm over his use of a poisonous pesticide.

TOLLY FARM

1980–1   Enoch and Grace Tolly,
           Naomi Tolly,
           Hannah Tolly

Enoch Tolly was another bad-tempered tenant farmer who totally dominated his family – wife Grace and daughters Naomi and Hannah. In 1980, cantankerous Enoch had a row with Richard Anstey, NY Estates' manager in the village, who challenged him over his continued use of a poisonous pesticide.

When Hannah – as stubborn as her father – made clear her opposition to this practice, she moved out of the house, followed by her mother and sister, who hoped to persuade Enoch to accept Anstey's ultimatum to stop using the pesticide. It worked and the farmer's family returned home.

But their life was torn apart when Enoch died in a tractor accident in February 1981. As Grace struggled to keep the farm going, NY Estates gamekeeper Seth Armstrong helped by suggesting they hire former Home Farm cowman Daniel Hawkins to work there, but the family were forced to sell up the following year.

LOWER HALL FARM

1981–6   Clifford and Peggy Longthorn,
           Carol Longthorn,
           Andy Longthorn (1981–3)

After his arrival in Beckindale, Jackie Merrick soon made friends with Andy, son of farmer Clifford Longthorn. In 1981, the pair found stolen goods in a cottage in the village and Sgt MacArthur wrongly suspected them of being responsible for the crime.

Studious Andy was also the boyfriend of Jackie's sister, Sandie, but she had no qualms about also seeing agricultural student David Blackmore, who arrived in Beckindale in his flash car to help Joe Sugden at NY Estates, and unemployed mechanic Graham Jelks, who was often at the centre of trouble in the village.

Then, in 1983, Sandie fell pregnant and tried to keep secret the identity of the baby's father. In fact, Andy had plied Sandie with sherry at the vicarage,

Lower Hall Farm tenant Clifford Longthorn's son Andy is revealed to be the father of Sandie Merrick's illegitimate baby, which she gives away for adoption.

Old Bill Whiteley's son, agricultural sales rep Pete, caused a scandal in Beckindale by bedding teenager Rachel Hughes on her 18th birthday in 1989. He eventually ended the affair and moved to Birmingham with wife Lynn, a former milk recorder.

But the couple returned the following year and Pete started seeing Rachel again. Tragically, however, he was killed when Rachel's mother, Kate Sugden, accidentally ran him over in the dark on the Robblesfield road. Lynn gave birth to baby son Peter Jr on the very day of Pete's father's funeral, in August 1990. Kate was subsequently jailed for manslaughter.

The following year, Lynn had another death to cope with – that of Pete's father, Bill, with whom she and her husband had lived at Whiteley's Farm. During her widowhood in Beckindale, Lynn made romantic conquests of both Rachel's ex-fiancé, Michael Feldmann, and her stepfather, Joe Sugden, but she failed in her attempt to seduce Joe's brother, Jack.

When Archie Brooks moved in as a non-paying lodger, he proved the perfect babysitter. But, when he started childminding for single dad Nick Bates, Lynn charged him rent of £20 a week. Eventually, in 1992, she threw him out.

Michael Feldmann and troublesome Lorraine Nelson, daughter of Woolpack barmaid Carol, lodged at the farmhouse for a while – but both spelled trouble. Michael was on bail before being jailed for taking part in a robbery at Home Farm. Lorraine stole money from Lynn's handbag, although it emerged that her problems stemmed from her father abusing her as a child.

Lynn's occasional shows of enterprise included running the Woolpack wine bar and a country club at Frank Tate's Holiday Village. Even Beckindale's worst disaster, the plane crash of 1993, was seen by the increasingly cynical young widow as a source of profit. She lured tabloid newspaper reporter Gavin Watson into her bed in return for pointing him in the direction of human-interest stories. But he disappeared as soon as the event ceased to be newsworthy.

where Jackie was staying while bailed on a charge of arson, and then made love to her for the first and last time.

When Jackie found out, he gave Andy a black eye. The boy's father told Sandie that Andy would marry her, give up his studies and take over Lower Hall Farm when he came of age. But Sandie turned down the offer and had baby daughter Louise quietly in Scotland after Andy left home for university.

Clifford, wife Peggy and daughter Carol were evicted from Lower Hall Farm in 1986, when NY Estates wanted to make use of the land, and moved to Lincoln. A year later, 30 acres of that land was bought by Harry Mowlem for his quarry.

WHITELEY'S FARM

1989–94   Bill Whiteley (1989–91),
          Pete (1989–90) and Lynn Whiteley,
          Peter Whiteley Jr (1990–4)
Lodgers: Archie Brooks (1990–2),
          Michael Feldmann (1993),
          Lorraine Nelson (1993)

By then Lynn had few friends left in Beckindale, and on meeting sheep-shearer Sven Olsen in 1994 she took the opportunity to start a new life with him in Australia.

Old Bill Whiteley finds trouble on the doorstep of Whiteley's Farm when son Pete has an affair with teenager Rachel Hughes.

HAWKINS COTTAGE

1993–6   Dr Bernard and Angharad McAllister, Luke McAllister, Jessica McAllister

The arrival of the McAllister family from Surrey in 1993 brought with it the village's first GP in many years. Back in 1973, Dr Grant left Clare Scott in charge of the Beckindale practice when he retired. She left in 1977 and Dr Jacobs took over until his retirement in 1985, when Dr Sharma stepped in. But villagers subsequently had to travel to Hotten if they needed to see a doctor.

Dr Bernard McAllister was returning to work as a GP after cutbacks at his London hospital made his chances of becoming a consultant slim. His wife, Angharad, became deputy head of Hotten Comprehensive.

One of Bernard's first tasks was to deal with the aftermath of the horrific plane crash over the village in December 1993. He was also instrumental in administering the money collected by the Disaster Fund.

But the family's time in the village was marred by the presence of their teenage children Luke and Jessica at a rave party the following year when Ben

Dingle died in a fight with motorcycle-mad Luke. As Luke faced manslaughter or murder charges, it emerged that a rare condition had caused Ben's death. But the Dingles swore revenge and fought with Luke outside Hotten Comprehensive.

When Angharad discovered that Tina Dingle was in her class and, at the same time, Kathy Tate became obsessed with Bernard following the break-up of her second marriage, the McAllisters decided to leave Emmerdale after little more than a year in the village.

However, Luke refused to go and a devastated Jessica ran off with boyfriend Biff Fowler, losing her virginity to him in a night of passion. In the event, she decided to join her parents as they left, although she returned later to find that Luke had fallen for Tina Dingle, who claimed to be pregnant by him. A bewildered Betty Eagleton oversaw events at Hawkins Cottage in her capacity as housekeeper.

The phantom pregnancy proved to be Tina's way of getting revenge for her brother's death. After agreeing to marry Luke, she jilted him at the altar. Shortly afterwards, he bundled Tina into a van, sped off and crashed on a bend, killing himself. Tina escaped with her life but felt genuine remorse for her actions.

Bernard McAllister becomes Beckindale's first GP in many years when he arrives at Hawkins Cottage with teacher wife Angharad and children Luke and Jessica.

The Cairns family's time at Woodside Farm is short after Will discovers mother Becky trying to seduce vet Zoë Tate following her own unhappy time in Emmerdale.

WOODSIDE FARM

1997–8   Tony and Becky Cairns,
Will Cairns, Emma Cairns

Jack and Sarah Sugden bought Woodside Farm after the second Emmerdale farmhouse, previously known as Hawthorn Cottage, was bulldozed to make way for the access road to Demdyke Quarry in January 1997. But they never lived there, eventually deciding that the work needed, including underpinning, was too costly.

Looking to offload the property without losing money, Jack sold it to Tony and Becky Cairns for £50,000 more than he had paid and moved into a working farm instead. Tony then discovered that the work would cost another £50,000.

Grudgingly, Tony was persuaded by Becky to accept Jack and Sarah's offer of renting Tenant House, which belonged to Jack's mother, Annie, until Woodside Farm was habitable. The couple finally moved in with son Will and daughter Emma in November 1997.

However, they were on the move again the following year after Tony accepted a job in Düsseldorf as head of outdoor activities for a top European executive training scheme.

Right Alex lords it over Oakwell Hall until fleeing over his part in Linda Fowler's death.

OAKWELL HALL

1997–8   Lord Alex Oakwell (1997),
Lady Tara Oakwell

Young Lord Alex Oakwell proved to be one of Kim Tate's first business associates after she inherited the Home Farm estate from husband Frank in 1997. The gauche aristocrat saw the opportunity to get an injection of cash into his ailing stud business – and bed Kim.

However, Alex was engaged to upper-crust Tara Cockburn, who was interested only in his title. Kim did all she could to prevent Alex marrying Tara and, when Tara became Lady Oakwell, she refused to be his mistress.

Kim eventually accepted Steve Marchant's proposal of marriage. At their engagement party in October 1997, drug-taking Alex chatted up married vet's receptionist Linda Fowler, took her for a late-night car ride and crashed. He fled the scene of the accident, leaving Linda there to die, and when he left the country to avoid prosecution, Kim and Tara helped in the cover-up. Linda's grief-stricken father, Ned Glover, later set Oakwell Hall's stables on fire.

Tara was shocked when Alex reappeared in February 1998, but she agreed to leave the country with him. It was an even greater shock when he stole her diamonds and left without her.

Always more business-minded than her estranged husband, Tara then joined Chris Tate in financing Tony Cairns's activities centre, based at Home Farm's Holiday Village. She demonstrated her shrewdness by buying a majority shareholding in Home Farm during 1998.

Index